entrepreneurs and for those wishing to
is trepreneurship. The book is written in
many interesting stories that catch one's
trate Ayurveda concepts and the stories
with Greek mythology and more'—Anu
teapmygenome

eneur since 1999. Despite this experience,
en is an FMCG product, I requested Gopal to
d I did this. There's so much for start-ups to
beautifully brought out in Section 2, where I
r 8. If you are involved with Indian start-ups
read this book'—K. Vaitheeswaran, co-founder,
epreneur, referred to as 'father of e-commerce in
hor

wise men, have presented a well-researched and
current entrepreneurial ecosystem in India. They
, that there is a need to rise above the hubris of mere
easure of success. There are many good habits that
in order to build a sustainable enterprise. This book
r the secret sauce for real success. They also debate the
ecosystem for India than the one adopted from Silicon
tial read for entrepreneurs and all the other stakeholders
–Pravin Gandhi, founder director and managing partner,

or business leader will be able to put this book down. It is
at storytelling, business wisdom and pragmatic thinking. As
r and the founder of a technology company, I can vouch for
e authors bring a uniquely informed and exciting perspective
must-read'—Pradeep Kar, founder, chairman and managing
roland Limited

h the wisdom from two corporate veterans, bringing their own
om two different career and entrepreneurial paths, this book is
rad for any start-up that wants to learn the art of living a long
py life. Corporate Ayurveda, or the art and science of long life for
ations, is what is packed into this handy book. While the book is
with stories from the Indian start-up world and big corporates, it
ontains numerous references to management concepts, all together
g it a compelling read'—Ambi Parameswaran, independent brand
and bestselling author

Wisdom for Start-ups
from Grown-ups

DISCOVERING
CORPORATE
AYURVEDA

R. GOPALAKRISHNAN
and R. NARAYANAN

PORTFOLIO
PENGUIN

An imprint of Penguin Random House

PORTFOLIO

USA | Canada | UK | Ireland | Australia
New Zealand | India | South Africa | China

Portfolio is part of the Penguin Random House group of companies
whose addresses can be found at global.penguinrandomhouse.com

Published by Penguin Random House India Pvt. Ltd
7th Floor, Infinity Tower C, DLF Cyber City,
Gurgaon 122 002, Haryana, India

Penguin
Random House
India

First published in Portfolio by Penguin Random House India 2021

10 9 8 7 6 5 4 3 2 1

The views and opinions expressed in this book are the authors' own and the
facts are as reported by them which have been verified to the extent possible,
and the publishers are not in any way liable for the same.

ISBN 9780670091539

Typeset in Adobe Garamond Pro by Manipal Technologies Limited, Manipal
Printed at Replika Press Pvt. Ltd, India

www.penguin.co.in

MIX
Paper from
responsible sources
FSC® C016779

To our families, for their support throughout this time-consuming project

Contents

Preface

We are business professionals. We were fortunate to study at premier institutes such as the Indian Institute of Technology (IIT) and the Indian Institute of Management (IIM). We believe that experience trumps theoretical knowledge. Through almost a hundred years of collective business experience, we have developed perspectives on start-ups, grown-ups and the connections between them. And since our experience profiles have been different, they inform our perspectives—consolidated in this book—in their own unique way.

I, R. Gopalakrishnan (Gopal), have spent my half-century-long career in two large corporations, Unilever and Tata, both of which should rightly be thought of as grown-ups. Although these companies have the image of being stable and long established, both embed entrepreneurial new ventures and start-ups within their wombs. I had the opportunity to participate in and initiate such ventures during my career.

I, R. Narayanan (Naru), began my career in well-established companies—Coca-Cola and Nestlé—followed by considerable experience in the advertising business. Thereafter, the entrepreneurship bug bit me. Since the 1980s, I have been deeply involved with start-ups. I founded and ran a company to make and market Big Fun, a chewing gum. My next venture was to create a machine or a business system to dispense dosa—just like a hamburger—an offering which I branded as Dosa King. After sequentially exiting the two start-ups, where I learnt many lessons, I became a passionate participant in angel investing and mentoring.

Therefore, both of us have rich experience in corporate management and entrepreneurship—varied, exciting, educative and, above all, complementary.

We are blood brothers, just one year apart in age, so it was natural that we would meet quite often. Apart from reminiscing about childhood, family incidents and common friends, we also discussed the experiences throughout our careers, usually in a desultory manner. And one such conversation about a professional matter resulted in a difference of opinion, which sparked the idea for this book.

If start-ups are one side of the coin, representing new-generation business, grown-ups are the other side of the coin. The physical, psychological and emotional connection between start-ups and grown-ups is important to the economy and to society. Start-ups and grown-ups are connected delicately, a bit like the corpus callosum that connects the right and left parts of the human brain.

If one follows the public commentaries and perceptions about long-standing companies, it would seem like the last few nails are being hammered into their coffins in light of the rapidly growing start-ups. One almost imagines these companies to be on Easter Island, the once-prosperous island inhabited by the Polynesians, who went extinct in an apparently mysterious manner.

Atomic scientist Niels Bohr had appropriately said, 'We assume that the opposite of a truth is a falsehood, whereas it could well be another truth.' The perception about large companies is only partially true, if at all. Human advancement does not take place along a linear path. It does so more along the rim of a rotating wheel. Previous events tend to come right back, creating patterns. This eternal truth forms an important basis for this book.

As regards the structure of the book, we have divided it into two sections.

Section 1 is focused on start-ups.

Under this, Chapter 1 explores the motivations among entrepreneurs, the calling that draws them to 'the wild'. In Chapter 2, we narrate the stories of nine start-ups. We have tried to avoid hagiographies or describing the determinants of individual success to steer clear of adulatory narratives, which seem to be the norm. We tell these stories to elucidate the pulls and pressures, the compelling desire to do well with whatever they have chosen and some of their near-death experiences and lessons. Chapter 3 covers the changing landscape of entrepreneurship in India and dwells on the factors that allow start-ups to imagine the innovative business models they embark upon. Chapter 4 considers certain verticals, only as examples, to illustrate the analytical and intuitive frameworks through which start-ups are able to think about their business models. This chapter argues that the marketing functions, including demand assessment and customer preferences, receive scant attention from start-up founders.

Section 2 focuses on grown-ups.

Using the human metaphor, Chapter 5 underlines the importance of building corporate ventures that have long lives to their founders and leaders. Chapter 6 addresses the question of whether companies resemble human beings, specifically in the matter of life lessons. Are the life lessons of grown-ups relevant to start-ups? We believe the answer is in the affirmative. So, how can these life lessons be shared? Chapter 7 reviews some of the generic growing-up challenges of companies. Learning important lessons from those companies that have mastered the art of long life is a subject captured in Chapter 8. Chapter 9 wraps up the narrative about grown-ups by reviewing interesting anecdotes and stories of some grown-up companies.

Finally, Chapter 10 summarizes the discussions in the book and reveals the 'secret sauce' by summarizing the discussions in the book and threading the wisdom from grown-ups with the dilemmas of start-ups.

On the whole, this book seeks to restate basic truths as to what constitutes vigorous and healthy business companies with a long life. We hope that we have been able to distil some of the timeless wisdom of long-life companies into something meaningful for start-ups.

Whom This Book Will Interest

The book is aimed at leaders and budding managers who are/will be charged with taking care of the health and growth of their companies. But any person who is interested in understanding the nuances of institutional good health and longevity will find this book very useful. The book is also aimed at the entrepreneur. After all, entrepreneurs are like 'young parents' and must be made aware of and encouraged to practise what might give their creations a long life. The target reader is anybody who is interested in knowing how to transform their companies into long-living (*deerga ayush*) companies. Companies are like human beings insofar as their creator desperately wants it to grow into a successful adult and to live a long and fruitful life.

SECTION 1

Start-ups

1

The Call of the Wild

This chapter seeks to take the reader on a breezy ride through the tumultuous thoroughfares of business and markets that created the technology-based start-ups over the last thirty years. While revisiting these apparently chaotic times, the reader will encounter the players. The authors do not seek to judge the players or their ventures. In any case, the last word has not been said about either. The book merely presents the challenges and the responses of the players to recreate the tyranny and excitement of the entrepreneurial revolution in India.

The Y2K Problem

As the world awaited breathlessly the year 2000, the Y2K bug posed a huge problem. All the PCs in the world had been designed with one common flaw. It was projected that this problem in the coding of computerized systems would create havoc in computers and computer networks worldwide. And this was slated to occur at 12.01 a.m. on 1 January 2000. The word was out well before that date, of course, and the world went on a frenzy of hiring programmers to prevent the problem from occurring.

The net beneficiary was India, which was well positioned to fill the demand that cropped up. When the world woke up on 1 January 2000, the problem seemed to have magically rectified itself and, apart from select and isolated malfunctions, the world did not miss a beat. The consequences for India were not as severe as initially thought.

The previous decade had seen a huge and frantic recruitment binge, and it appeared that only the Indian subcontinent could fill that gap, as thousands of programmers were recruited for either onshore work in the US or offshore work from India. The years that followed turned out to be boom years for the growth of the IT services industry, as the country's education infrastructure hastened to take advantage of this opportunity.

The Dot-Com Boom and Thereafter

Around the same time as Y2K, the Internet was coming of age. Through a stroke of good fortune, India was churning out a large number of engineers, who walked right into the Internet age. And the Internet had also democratized entrepreneurial activity in the post-Y2K phase.

Capital, which had always been in short supply, suddenly became increasingly available and started finding its way to good ideas. Nearly anybody who had a good idea could raise capital. And we have several examples of entrepreneurs of Indian origin who rode the wave of the first dot-com boom and went down with the bust that followed in 2001. Ask Kanwal Rekhi, an Indian–American businessman, entrepreneur, angel investor and venture capitalist. Today he serves as the managing director of Inventus Capital Partners. Kanwal tells us that in the early '90s, when Indians went to venture capitalists to attempt a fundraiser, they faced a peculiar situation time and again: 'You are an Indian. What do you know about being an entrepreneur? You should be working for others.' Kanwal goes on to say that several Indians in the US got together and asked themselves, 'If this is how *we* are being viewed, how bad would it be for Indian entrepreneurs back home?'

And so was born the non-profit organization The IndUS Entrepreneurs (TiE), an association of entrepreneurs and wannabe-entrepreneurs seeking to serve entrepreneurs all over the world. Today, TiE is represented by over 11,000 members across nineteen countries. Several TiE chapters have been at the forefront of giving birth to early angel-investing groups. The Indian Angel Network, the Mumbai Angels and the Chennai Angels—three of the most active angel groups in the country—owe their origins to TiE.

Kanwal admits that even in their wildest imagination, the founders of TiE never thought that it would become a global network and find representation in nineteen countries—and that too all within thirty years of its inception. Nearly all technology entrepreneurs in India have associated with TiE or one of the angel groups at some stage or the other. It would not be an exaggeration to say that TiE has done much for the entrepreneurial ecosystem across the globe. Along with the Indian hardware and software industry associations of the technology industry, Manufacturers' Association of Information Technology (MAIT) and National Association of Software and Service Companies (NASSCOM), TiE has done much to place India on the world map of technology.

Seeds of Entrepreneurship

These days, there are at least one hundred thousand software engineers every year in India who dream of becoming entrepreneurs. It is a long and perilous journey for them. Perhaps roughly two thousand out of the one hundred thousand in our view will get funded. However, within just a few decades, there will be two million aspiring entrepreneurs and the ecosystem will have to cater to their expectations.

Speculating about the future, by 2025 hopefully, half a million entrepreneurs will get funded and, assuming an average employment of ten each, they will generate annual employment of five million. One of the authors of this book, Naru, recollects talking to the joint secretary at the Ministry of Education in New Delhi in 1982, where the latter had said, 'There is no doubt that India will be a software powerhouse within the next ten years.' He was a bit ahead of his times. By 2000, India had truly achieved this status. Arguably, today, over a million Indians are employed as software professionals in the US alone. And we estimate another three million employed in India to serve markets outside India.

Dreams, Millionaires and Unicorns

Ask any nineteen-year-old engineering student in Rajahmundry (Rajamahendravaram, Andhra Pradesh) or Trichy (Tiruchirappalli, Tamil Nadu) about their life's ambition. There is a high probability that their short-term dream is to graduate and get employment in one of the big five—Tata Consultancy Services (TCS), Infosys, Wipro, Hindustan Computers Limited (HCL) or Tech Mahindra. Thirty years ago, it would have been Intel, Hewlett-Packard (HP), Cisco or one of the many early multinationals that had anchored in India. But today, Indian powerhouses are perceived to offer as much, perhaps more, to the beginner.

Two years into their job, ask any engineer working in a software firm as to what his life's ambitions are and the answer is likely to be, 'Get a US/UK posting.' Eight years into his job, the ambition of every engineer is to start his own company. Incidentally, that is equally true for professionals in India as well as those in the US.

And, in a way, it all started with a guy called Sabeer Bhatia.

One could argue that among the many things that Sabeer did, he also brought the world's attention to the technopreneurial brilliance of Indian engineers. While the world was still looking for software solutions and email clients, Sabeer and his friend, Jack Smith, conceived of a web-based email solution called Hotmail.

They raised a mere $300,000 in 1996 to start Hotmail. By the end of 1997, Sabeer had sold Hotmail to Microsoft for $400 million.

Truly, Sabeer Bhatia is the original poster boy of Indian tech entrepreneurs in the Internet age. While Bollywood contemplated making a movie portraying the Sabeer Bhatia story, he had already risen and had started fading from public memory. But he could not fade from the memory or imagination of the Indian engineer. Every Indian engineer wanted to be like Sabeer Bhatia, and Sabeer had established that it was possible. Until then, Indian entrepreneurs could dream about building complex software systems for enterprises. But Sabeer was single-handedly responsible for opening the window to the creation of products for consumers, instead of solutions for enterprises. Sabeer was, for a long time, also the poster boy of Indian success in the US and became an icon for others to follow. And several did. Both in India and in the US.

The arrival of the dotcom era in the late 1990s presented an irresistible opportunity to Pradeep Kar, born with entrepreneurial blood coursing through his veins. As the founder and CMD of Microland and a pioneer in the networking space, he had his finger on the pulse of the technology business in the country. With breathtaking speed, he launched many Internet-based companies, one after the other: Planetasia.com became India's first Internet professional services provider; ITspace.com was India's first tech portal; Indya.com made its mark as a consumer portal that created several historic landmarks; Media2India.net addressed the need for managing online advertising; and Kar's company partnered with US-based Penton Media to launch the world's largest Internet conference called 'India Internet World'.

Indya.com was his masterstroke. His investors included John Sculley, the ex-CEO of Apple Computers and PepsiCo; Vinod Khosla, co-founder of Sun Microsystems and renowned venture capitalist; Rajat Gupta, the then CEO of McKinsey; Yogen Dalal, managing partner of Mayfield Ventures; and Ram Shriram, board member of Google. Rupert Murdoch wrote a cheque for US$ 50 million for a one-third share in Indya. The company was valued at Rs 7,500 million even before it was launched!

On 16 April 2000, a huge banner appeared on the front pages of the *Times of India*, brashly announcing that 'India Changes Its Name Today'. It heralded the launch of Indya.com, simultaneously changing the advertising business. Never before had the old lady of Bori Bunder (as the *Times of India* is fondly known in deference to its vintage) set aside its entire front page for an advertisement. Kar admits it was a seriously bold leap he took, almost without looking. "We had to apologize for saying that India changes its name today," he says. "The government took objection to the very idea!" Indya. com showed the nation what a multi-faceted portal could be and it set the pace for the Internet economy in India. It partnered with several startups in the travel and ticketing space. Many of them have gone on to establish themselves as the face of digital India. Many of the employees of Indya.com refused to take up regular jobs when the portal was forced to shut down during the dotcom bust.

Today these entrepreneurs are behind organizations like the award-winning financial advisory planning company International Money Matters, local search company Just Dial (who has doubled up as an early investor in Dunzo), and the founder of Runner for Life that has been growing and supporting the marathoners community since 2005. Indya.com will go down in history as the Internet business that inspired the entrepreneurial community.

Enter Junglee

Among the many that were perhaps inspired by Sabeer were four IIT/Stanford alumni. Venky Harinarayan, Ashish Gupta, Anand Rajaraman and Rakesh Mathur came together to start a company called Junglee. Essentially a price-comparison site, Junglee was ahead of its time in the e-commerce world and was promptly acquired by Amazon for $240 million in 1998.

Within just two years from the time of Junglee's acquisition, the four Junglee co-founders came together once again to back HyperTrack, with offices in Delhi and San Francisco. HyperTrack provided 'location as a service' and enabled companies like Swiggy and Zomato to pinpoint the location of the delivery to the end customer.

All four of them went on to become angel investors and/or venture capitalists, with a strong emphasis on Indian start-ups and the Indian e-commerce ecosystem. In addition, they provided mentorship to start-ups from India and to the Silicon Valley investors. And this trend has been followed by others such as Vinod Dham and Kanwal Rekhi.

The Amazing Yahoo

In the San Francisco Bay area, Yahoo began as part of a list of other websites that Jerry Yang and David Filo started in the proverbial garage. It wasn't even a garage; it was a trailer. Known initially as 'Jerry and David's Guide to the World Wide Web', the list consisted of hundreds of websites that had been manually classified into relevant headings. By early 1995, traffic had grown to several million hits per day. Stanford University, which had provided them access to their servers, asked them to shift to servers of their own, for which, of course, they required money.

In January 1995, Yahoo.com was formally registered and Sequoia Capital, an American venture capital firm, put up $2 million for as much as 25 per cent of the company. And inevitably, the two founders gave up the pursuit of their PhDs at Stanford and took this up full-time. And what a golden ride it turned out to be for them!

After manually indexing thousands of websites, Yahoo sought to automate the process. They partnered with Inktomi, a California-based company that provided software for Internet service providers and, thereafter, with Google, in its early days. In 2004, Yahoo went independent.

By 2001, there were several wannabe search engines, like AltaVista, also in the running, and Google started moving to prominence in 2004. Notwithstanding the current status of either

Yahoo or Google, it is useful to remember that at its peak Yahoo had a 70 per cent market share of all searches over the Internet. As an integrated portal with its own search function, Yahoo seemed invincible in its time.

By the end of 1995, Masayoshi Son of SoftBank flew down to California to meet the Yahoo founders. SoftBank initially invested $2 million for a 5 per cent stake. But shortly after that, Son agreed to invest $100 million more, for a 41 per cent combined stake in Yahoo. Considering how the world was in March 1996, it was a gutsy thing to do. Yang flew to Japan at Son's request and started Yahoo, Japan. In April 1996, Yahoo went public on NASDAQ, and investors valued the company at $850 million. At the time, Yahoo had just $1.4 million in annual revenue and losses of over $600,000. The dot-com boom was in full bloom. Within three years, both Filo and Yang became billionaires. Their success propelled SoftBank to list on the primary board of the Tokyo Stock Exchange in January 1998, making Masayoshi Son a billionaire.

The development of new Indian start-ups and their fortunes in those years made for an exciting trajectory. The way the early e-commerce companies came up and survived makes for a Robert Ludlum-like thriller narrative. What made these entrepreneurs undertake these journeys and what motivated them is something that needs to be appreciated by replaying the events in their contexts.

The next chapter brings together nine spirited stories. As the reader gets immersed in these stories, it will become evident that it is no accident that the path to reach global scale is arduous, one that can easily take more than a decade. For people associated with start-ups who are reading this book, hopefully this will be an awakening. The Indian ecosystem is still distant from high-velocity acquisitions and mergers. So, as you set out to become a serious entrepreneur, it might be a good idea to fortify yourself to becoming a long-distance runner.

The other point that we would like to highlight to the reader is that the right mindset and personality find eventual success. To put it softly, it seems that a little humility helps, although the laborious journey will also beat you into submission. A good deal of focus helps. If you are thinking day in and day out about your business and its position in the marketplace, then there is good reason to assume that you will find business revelations frequently. That will help in making you successful, as you can see from the examples above.

And, finally, it is good to have an open mind about the strategies deployed and to frequently examine and re-examine them for refinement. Meanwhile, also be open to adjacent opportunities. These opportunities may be stepping stones towards your original goal, not necessarily a deviation!

The call of the unknown and hidden treasures have always attracted a breed of entrepreneurs. The current state of technology in the world can set your heart aflutter. The gains look huge but can mislead you into making high-risk decisions without fully contemplating the implications. History has been replete with such opportunities, and entrepreneurs and business-minded people have not hesitated to beg, borrow and steal, or even risk their lives and that of others across a wide cross section of vocations and industries, to take advantage of such opportunities. Some of such instances will be touched upon in this book as we trace the way the world has progressed from time immemorial. And in a sense, it seems that it is no different today compared to what it was thousands of years ago. And the ability to see that makes for humility!

Now on to the next chapter, about nine very interesting and true stories of real start-ups.

2

Ceuta and Cape Bojador Stories

Ceuta and Cape Bojador

In 1415, Portugal had won independence from Castile (Spain) and should have been at peace with its travails and the world.[1] The restless royal family had an urge to do something that would promote trade and prosperity for Portugal. The king was attracted to Ceuta, a small Mumbai-shaped strip of land between Spain and Morocco in the Mediterranean. Ceuta was the epicentre of the camel trade to and from Europe into the sub-Saharan trade route all the way to the Sahel kingdom. The king's son, Prince Henry, was strongly in favour of the Ceuta adventure, much against the advice of the court elders. Perhaps he knew that, as the third son, his chances of succeeding the king were almost zero. A well-planned and -executed maritime conquest might earn him a place in history.

After detailed planning, on 26 July 1415, Prince Henry and his fleet set sail for Ceuta. The defence by Ceuta's governor, Sala bin Sala, was quickly overcome, and Prince Henry gained full

---

[1] Jeffery Garten, *Silk to Silicon*, India: Tranquebar Press, 2015.

control of Portugal's first overseas colony, marking the beginning of several centuries of European maritime adventure.

After fifteen years, around the 1430s, Prince Henry sensed an irresistible urge to go beyond Cape Bojador. In the popular imagination, Cape Bojador, on the west African coast, was the point of no return. Many expeditions before had come to grief, and legend had it that sea monsters cooked intruders in the 'boiling sea waters' and ate them up. Prince Henry got his squire, Gil Eannes, to study the terrain in detail and the prince somehow persuaded Eannes to undertake the voyage to circumvent Cape Bojador, which meant 'the bulging cape'.

The results of these breakthroughs in sea navigation are recorded in history. If Ceuta was Prince Henry's most formative experience, then Cape Bojador may be considered his most important.

Every entrepreneur has his or her own Ceuta and Cape Bojador. As the reader goes through the narratives that follow, they will find it instructive to identify each entrepreneur's equivalent of the dangerous capes and landings along the ocean.

Nine Stories

There are many books and articles about various Indian start-ups. They have, no doubt, produced a rich tapestry of stories, available through secondary research. In addition, there are personal interviews of and anecdotes from the authors, and these can add to the intricacies of the warp and weft. Due to his engagement with the resurgent start-up world, Naru has myriad connections. His insights have influenced the perspectives in several of the stories that follow.

1. Sify: Timing Matters

Naru has fond admiration for Ramaraj, known as Ram. 'Ram has deservedly been felicitated by Indian Institute of Mass Communication (IIMC). He is the backbone of the entrepreneurial movement in Chennai. A former president of TiE Chennai, and an early founding member of TCA (The Chennai Angels), Ram is omnipresent at all major business functions in and around Chennai. He and I share a great interest in the start-up ecosystem as well as in reading Lee Child. Ram is highly approachable, and I have seen this characteristic from his early days in Siva Computers, Chennai.'

In India, sometime in the late '90s, the government woke up to the need of bandwidth and the emerging presence of the Internet across the globe. Not wanting to be left out, the government enunciated a policy and invited entrepreneurs and businessmen to bid for and acquire Internet licences. Clearly, after the launch of the telecom policy and mobile licences, ISP (Internet service provider) licences seemed the last big-time opportunity that was not to be missed. News of the unreasonable valuations was just making its way to the Indian shores, and it truly appeared magical. Amazon had already made its presence felt, and Yahoo had already demonstrated that it did not require profitability to list on NASDAQ. It required hubris and belief. Amazon listed in 1997 and opened at $18 per share price. The reader may also know that the dot-com bust days must have been trying for Amazon. But the stock market had clearly embraced the Internet.

Over 600 companies in India obtained licences as ISPs, and there was a mad rush to market as the stories of Yahoo and Amazon abounded. What would happen to the traditional store? Is it really possible to displace the *kirana* outlet? Is India not a 'touch and feel' market? These and other such typical queries, several of which are relevant even today, after two decades, were on the minds of thousands of citizens.

In 1999, Infosys, already a BSE-listed company, took a bold step of listing shares on NASDAQ. NASDAQ was being observed very carefully by several companies, listed as well as non-listed, as a bold way to raise funds. Over ninety-eight Israeli ISPs had already been listed on NASDAQ, and several Chinese companies too. Infosys had already paved the way for others from India to follow.

Infosys became the first Indian company to list on NASDAQ. Sify, the NASDAQ abbreviation for Satyam Infoway, was the second Indian company to list on NASDAQ, and the first Internet company to do so. The change of the company name to Sify came much later, in 2004.

Sify had obtained its ISP licence and launched in the marketplace with the US company Compuserve as its partner. Sify was primarily focused on the B2B market, and Compuserve brought several of its global clients so they could become customers of Sify in India. Thereafter, demand for data centres from corporates also grew, and although Sify was not making profits, it was sailing along, acquiring corporate customers at regular intervals. But clearly, the message that Sify was receiving was that it was the B2C business that had the hype and reflected the opportunity, so far as valuations were concerned. Moreover, Sify was running out of money and needed to do something quickly. Remember that Infosys had already taken the path and helped set a precedence and government policies had been somewhat defined.

The move from the idea to the actual listing on NASDAQ was one mad rush, and Sify listed at a valuation of $350 million. At that time, Chinese companies were listing in billions of dollars. The situation was tense and they needed to show solidarity and meticulously follow a plan.

Within seven months, there needed to be a change of merchant banker to Merrill Lynch for the IPO, as it became increasingly clear that the boutique merchant banker Donaldson, Lufkin and Jenrette (DLJ) would not be able to deliver on the time schedule that Sify needed. DLJ cooperated with the transition and shared the reports with Merrill Lynch. As in other cases, luck also played a major role once critical decisions had been made in a timely manner.

Looking at Yahoo and how the market was receiving consumer Internet companies, Sify knew that the market would assign respect to companies that were in the B2C business. ISPs and portals from China were listed and valued at much higher levels than Indian companies.

But while the government had issued licences for ISPs, access to the Internet was still by dial-up. Moreover, at the time, the total penetration of personal computers (PCs) into households was less than one million. So, while Sify recognized that the stock market favoured B2C players, the task ahead for a B2C company was formidable. A huge amount of money was being incurred post-listing to bring about a consumer revolution in the adoption of the Internet among consumers.

Meanwhile, Compuserve got acquired by AOL.com, a largely B2C company. Sify had revenues from B2B but now needed to step out and make their presence felt in the B2C segment.

Sify commenced with selling compact discs (CDs) for dial-up, a strategy that had worked extremely well for AOL (America Online) in the US and arguably accounted for its unprecedented success then. Recognizing that there was a paucity of PCs in households, Sify laid out an ambitious programme of establishing 5000 branded Internet cafes nationally as soon as possible—and they managed to do it within eighteen months. But notwithstanding the efforts being made and despite the immaculate execution, the truth of the matter was that funds were drying up again.

But the global dot-com boom was still on the ascent and it seemed a good time to go out and raise a second round on NASDAQ. Sify raised $150 million in early 2000. So here was the classic trap—a slow uptake on the B2C business in spite of a considerable amount of investment made in the B2C market. The B2C business devoured so much money that the belief within Sify was that a bust-up was imminent. At the end of 2000, the expected dot-com bust did happen.

Early indicators were visible. Several dot-com companies did not survive to experience a second round of funding, while others closed down in the face of burn rates which did not even leave them two months of life. In addition to the B2C initiatives, Sify had invested in remote infrastructure management services and was about to go global with this service. An office had been opened in the US and staffing had just commenced when a trickle of the dot-com bust became a storm.

Sify had also acquired Cricinfo and Khiladi.com (the latter was started by Geet Sethi, the billiards champion) and the dot-com bust had started looking quite like an existential threat. So, while the Indian dot-com boom commenced with the acquisition of IndiaWorld Communications and the culmination of Y2K, the boom was short-lived. So, along with the global dot-com bust, there took place the Indian dot-com bust as well.

Sify then took a decision that would later be heralded as the marker for the Indian dot-com boom. Indiaworld.com was a very visible website that represented the nascent e-commerce business available in India. Sify acquired Indiaworld.com at an astronomical and unheard-of price, of Rs 500 crore, from Rajesh Jain, who currently runs a company called Netcore Solutions.

The IndiaWorld acquisition by Sify in July 2000 resulted in an overnight increase in the market capitalization of Sify to $1.3 billion. The value kept going all the way up until it touched $8.5 billion.

Briefly for one day, as a watermark, the market cap of Sify overtook Reliance Industries, the darling of the BSE, and the company with the highest market cap in the country. And then the dot-com bust arrived. The end of the bust was barely in sight when the 9/11 attack happened and the world markets contracted. And a new battle for survival began.

In summary, Sify was acquired in 2005 by Raju Vegesna of Infinity Capital Ventures, who quickly shed the consumer business and consolidated the B2B activities of Sify. Sify is a profitable Rs 2500 crore company today, largely in the B2B business. They continue to be felicitated and celebrated every five years by NASDAQ.

An abundance of good fortune has contributed to Sify's success. It has stood the test of time and now is one of the largest ICT solution companies in India.

2. Flipkart and the Two Bansals

In 2007, as the world was already opening up to the idea of the online marketplace, the concept was still fairly unknown to the Indian customer. But with one of the largest expanding online populations in the world, electronic retail and largely the e-commerce industry had grown exponentially. Electronic retail, e-retail or e-tailing is the sale of goods and services via the Internet. These can include B2B or B2C methods. To build a successful online store, websites need to be engaging, easy to navigate and be able to keep up with customers' ever-changing demands. At this point in time, there were a few major players out there, Amazon and eBay to name a few, that had taken the Indian market by storm.

Setting up a dot-com company was easier than the conventional way of doing business. There were many reasons for this, among them lower start-up costs and a much larger customer base, thanks to the absence of geographical barriers, the strengthening of infrastructure to support a technology-friendly society, accessibility and less time consumption. Not only this, the Indian government and investors alike were aware of the power of the Internet and were backing these companies with infrastructure and finance respectively.

However, penetrating the Indian online marketplace had some challenges. A largely traditional society, Indians preferred to buy things they had examined through touch and feel rather than online, especially in large metro cities where there was a shop around every corner. The explosion of large malls and department stores also made things challenging. Overcoming the mental barrier of touch and feel was also a problem. Another big problem faced by online retail was logistics—transportation of materials and products from one place to another. Effective logistics had to play an important role in the operational success of online retailers.

From 2005 all the way to 2010, many players entered the Indian online space. And one of these was a company called Flipkart—and this is its story.

In October 2007, Flipkart was founded by Sachin Bansal and Binny Bansal (not relatives) from a two-bedroom apartment in Koramangala, Bangalore. Both alumni of IIT Delhi and former employees of online giant Amazon, they initially focused on online book sales with countrywide shipping, just like Amazon. Apart from that, there was also talk of being an online platform to compare prices. But in 2007, there weren't too many sites to compare. They both pondered for a few moments when they were both still with Amazon and finally decided to start an e-commerce site. Obviously there were problems, but Flipkart was able to close its first year with twenty successful deliveries, and it was officially in business.

With an initial investment of just about $8000, this venture grew into something neither Sachin nor Binny had envisioned. The founders were both passionate about providing tailor-made products specifically to Indian customers, creating an experience that could compete with the best in the industry and a robust back-end process—all prerequisites for an online business to be successful, and Flipkart seemed to know its way around. Of course, the massive growth of e-commerce in India did provide a well-timed lift to the company, which turned into a $100 million e-retailing favourite.

The years 2008 and 2009 were incredible years for Flipkart. With rapidly growing publicity, thanks to word of mouth, Flipkart opened its first office in Koramangala and launched 24/7 customer support to deal with the platform's ever-growing customer base. This was all in tune with the company's policy of 'Don't count your customers before they smile'.[2] Flipkart happily closed the financial year with upwards of 3000 customers served.

The year 2009 marked a year of firsts for the company. It hired its first full-time employee, Ambur Iyyappa, who would go on to become a millionaire. It was also the year when the meteoric growth

2   Ushamrita Choudhury, 'The Flipkart story', *The Hindu*, 12 July 2016, https://www.thehindu.com/features/magazine/the-flipkart-story/article3290735.ece

of the company caught the attention of the venture capital firm Accel Partners, which invested $1 million in the company. Flipkart then expanded its operations and opened offices in Mumbai and Delhi, increasing its headcount to 150. Another milestone crossed by Flipkart during this time was the booking of pre-orders for a book by Dan Brown called *The Lost Symbol*.

Another milestone year for the company was 2010, when they introduced cash on delivery (CoD) for customers. In fact, Flipkart was a pioneer of this mode of payment in India. Other sites soon followed suit, of course. But the option of CoD gave customers more trust in the site, and this led to a spike in the demand for goods. People obviously preferred to pay for things they could touch and feel and Flipkart mimicked the feeling of going to an actual department store and paying hard cash for your buys. All this was possible with the click of a mouse and at your doorstep.

In 2010, Flipkart hired an eager-eyed fresher from a prestigious B-school. He was one of Flipkart's first campus hires. His name was Vinoth Poovalingam and, at the time, the only experience he had was a summer internship stint at Britannia while pursuing his postgraduate degree at the Indian Institute of Management (IIM) Bangalore. Before IIM Bangalore, he had gone to IIT Madras and, unlike his friends, who all bagged fat corporate jobs, Poovalingam accepted an offer from Flipkart, a company barely a couple of years old that had just made the transition from books to other things. A young boy with dreams of becoming an entrepreneur himself, he thought that this job at Flipkart would pave the way for the future he had envisioned for himself.

As he joined Flipkart, a huge task was thrust into this youngster's hands. Building the Flipkart-owned, outbound logistics capability from scratch was no mean feat. It started as an optimistic local-area experiment but was soon turned into a trailblazing business for consumer logistics. This expanded rapidly and propelled Flipkart into its leadership position at the helm of India's nascent e-commerce market—all this out of Poovalingam's garage in Koramangala.

And this is how Ekart was born. Poovalingam cheekily jokes about the venture, 'I was its first general manager and delivery boy.'[3]

At the time of the launch of Ekart, B2B logistics was essentially the only kind of logistics support that existed. B2C was on nobody's to-do list at the time. Another venture that Flipkart dabbled in was the concept of cash on delivery, which was essentially unheard of. There were no partners ready to support this kind of payment system. And to collect small amounts from customers for deliveries was too expensive. Hence, Flipkart decided to do things on its own. Ekart and CoD were two projects that fell into Poovalingam's lap and, with the support and backing of senior management, he was able to get both projects off the ground without too much trouble.

On one strange occasion, the entire chain of command was sent a curt email by Sachin Bansal. Apparently, he had placed an order with them and it had not been delivered yet. Everyone scurried around trying to find the fault in the system and, on close examination, discovered that there was one. An absent-minded Sachin Bansal had provided an older address instead of the present one. There was a resounding sigh of relief throughout the system, and then it was back to business as usual.

Both Ekart and CoD changed the very landscape of Flipkart's journey towards success. Now, with orders increasing exponentially and people making sure they used their online social presence to sing praises of Flipkart, there seemed to be nothing the company couldn't handle.

Starting late in 2010, Flipkart acquired several companies on its path towards venturing into areas it hadn't dabbled in before. It acquired the Bangalore-based social discovery service weRead from Lulu.com. In the latter half of 2011, it acquired Mime360.com,

---

[3] Bijoy Venugopal, 'Vinoth Poovalingam, the Flipkart Fresher Who Built Ekart', Flipkartstories.com, 12 May 2017, https://stories.flipkart.com/vinoth-poovalingam-ekart/

related to digital content distribution. But the biggest and most noteworthy acquisition then happened in May 2012, when Flipkart acquired Myntra, an online fashion retailer, for about $20 billion. The site continues to operate as a parallel to Flipkart as a standalone subsidiary.[4]

Other significant events also happened during this time, like the start of a trend that was soon followed by other websites including Amazon. It was the exclusive launch and availability of a few smartphones that were not available on any other site or platform or even at physical retail stores. The high demand for the first phone launched, the Moto E, and the sudden surge in traffic to the website caused the Flipkart site to crash. However, this did not stop Flipkart as it continued to make other smartphones available for sale in the subsequent months.

On 6 October 2014, in honour of its anniversary and the Diwali season, Flipkart held its 'Big Billion Day' sale. The event generated a surge in traffic and led to a sale of $100 million in a short span of ten hours. The event, however, received a lot of criticism on social media as there were several technical difficulties as well as stock shortages.

In March 2015, Flipkart blocked access to its website for mobile users. This meant that users had to download the app to use Flipkart. A similar stunt was pulled with Myntra, which also followed the app-only model for a few months. But the reduction in sales (by 10 per cent) led to the idea being dropped and the site being up and running again.

In 2016, Flipkart acquired another online fashion retailer, Jabong, for $70 million. Flipkart and eBay attempted to get into some sort of a deal, whereby Flipkart would own eBay's Indian subsidiary as well as some form of cash investment from the company. The deal didn't pan out. Flipkart also attempted to acquire its main domestic competitor, Snapdeal, but that deal didn't come to fruition either.

---

[4] 'Big Deal: Flipkart Acquires Online Fashion Retailer Myntra', *Indian Express*, 22 May 2014, https://indianexpress.com/article/business/companies/flipkart-myntra-announce-merger/

In the same year, Sachin Bansal and Binny Bansal featured in *Time* magazine's list of 100 most influential people.

All in all, Flipkart was in a good place. It had overtaken Amazon as the leader in smartphone sales, leading by 33 per cent. The 'Big Billion Days' were especially significant for the company as they kept breaking their own records every year for smartphone sales.[5]

Walmart announced a $16 billion acquisition of Flipkart in August 2018.[4] The Competition Commission of India (CCI) approved the Walmart–Flipkart deal, and this move received mixed reactions. This was because traders all over the country feared that the deal would drive several small- and medium-scale retailers out of business.

The CCI, however, defended its stand on the deal and mentioned that the discounting practices of the website had to be dealt with separately. A lot of back and forth with Walmart and Flipkart, plus a little interference from eBay, which wanted to sell its stake back to the company, all culminated on 18 August 2018, when the deal was finally completed with Walmart. It would also provide $2 billion in equity funding to Flipkart.[6]

Post the acquisition by Walmart, Binny Bansal resigned to start his next venture.

All these problems don't seem to be stopping Flipkart, though. It calls 2017 a 'watershed year' with the rise in mobile- and fashion-related sales and the launch of private labels. Overall, the e-retail industry is only growing and is expected to rise by about 60 per cent in the next couple of years. How will Flipkart fare in all this? Only time will tell.

---

[5]   'Flipkart Beats Amazon to Become the Top Retailer of Smartphones Online', Business Insider, 22 November 2019, https://www.businessinsider.in/tech/news/flipkart-beats-amazon-as-indian-smartphone-sales-hit-a-record-high/articleshow/72182851.cms

[6]   'Walmart Completes Deal to Acquire 77% Stake in Flipkart, to Invest $2 Billion', *Times of India*, 18 August 2018, https://timesofindia.indiatimes.com/business/india-business/walmart-completes-deal-to-acquire-77-stake-in-flipkart-to-invest-2-billion/articleshow/65454382.cms

3. Snapdeal: Kunal Bahl and Rohit Bansal

This story exemplifies the tenacity of the founders to live through the travails of running a start-up, rise against all odds and witness a brief glimpse of success on an unheard-of scale, all followed by a sudden and abrupt drop. And then, lurching back, hopefully, to its position of pre-eminence. Here, the kudos should go to the promoters. Rise and fall is an everyday affair in the life of a start-up. No two days are ever the same. It's a cycle of thrills and chills.

Starting a business is never easy. This is even truer of India. Everyone who has ever been an entrepreneur will tell you the same thing. You need to work on your ideas, find capital and investors, and then work even harder to get results, or at least the kind of results you want. But once the problems are dealt with, all successful entrepreneurs will tell you the exact same thing again. It's the best feeling in the world to watch your ideas obtain recognition and then see your business take off. Yes, the ups and downs come with the territory but, as Sir Richard Branson, founder of the Virgin Group, so aptly put it, 'You don't learn to walk by following the rules, you learn by doing, and falling over, again and again.'[7]

In the story that follows, the reader is uniquely placed to see an early Internet explorer make its way to success—phenomenal success—and then come crashing down within weeks to what seems certain annihilation. But like the phoenix, Snapdeal appears to be rising from the ashes once again.

It rose from an offline business to an online marketplace with phenomenal growth, and a valuation of over $6.5 billion dollars to being on the verge of acquisition to its current status as it slowly and steadily crawls back into the black. But before we go into that, it is useful for us to understand the times in which all this is happening.

---

[7]   Jonah Peretti, 'Snapdeal Success Story', https://successstory.com/companies/snapdeal

This is the twenty-first century and technology makes its presence visible in the marketplace in a host of ways.

It was a time when land, labour and capital—in that order—were the three main factors of production. Land was never fungible, and labour called for huge efforts in transporting plantation workers to distant lands to work. Capital was usually contained within the country but with the formation of formal capital markets, capital too has become fungible. And an item like cash, which is usually in short supply, can, in the tech world, become abundantly available.

We attribute the origins of this abundant availability to what we refer to as the 'Silicon Valley model' (SVM). SVM can make capital available far beyond the understanding of mere human beings. It was usually publicly quoted of companies that seemed to touch such peaks, and that perhaps reflected the view of the market. But here the SVM is the collective view of a few heavy-duty investors. The outcome can be phenomenal valuations that defy any previously understood reasons. In the next chapter of this book, we have talked about SVM in some detail, but back to our main story.

Tech start-ups are known for their notoriously high failure rates—only two in hundred start-ups even get funded. This means that under 2 per cent of start-ups exist beyond the five-year mark. So what separates the unicorns from the horses? (For those in the dark, the term 'unicorn' is used to refer to a privately held start-up valued at over $1 billion). The term was coined by Aileen Lee, a venture capitalist. She chose the mythical animal to represent the statistical rarity of such highly valued ventures.[8]

A query can be raised here as to whether the status of being a unicorn is a sign of success of the venture. The answer to this question lies in asking ourselves: 'From whose point of view?' Remember that this valuation is not market-speak but a group of investors speaking. Investors who can cash out on their investment

---

[8] 'Unicorn (finance)', Wikipedia, https://en.wikipedia.org/wiki/Unicorn_ (finance)

profitably can obviously and clearly read their unicorn investment as a success. It is possible that the founders were also permitted an advantageous part exit, and they, too, can read this as a successful exit. All this would usually represent a handful of individuals or investors. For our purposes, we continue to believe that what constitutes success is the ability of the firm to provide a return on shareholder investment that is comparable to current market trends. And it is our hope, thesis and desire that success be also defined in terms of longevity of life.

The company that was started in February 2010 by Kunal Bahl and Rohit Bansal transitioned from an online couponing business to an online marketplace. We look at its founders, its successes and pitfalls in its ongoing journey and the lessons it has learnt along the way.[9]

Schoolmates, both from Delhi Public School, Bansal and Bahl hit upon the idea of opening up an online coupon start-up to share information on daily deals and coupons, designed along the lines of Groupon.

In an interview in 2014, Bahl reportedly said that he knew his 'life was going to be a series of failures'. And going by the tumultuous journey that his company has faced, it seems the prophecy is fulfilling itself. He also said that these failures would help 'build character' and, going by how Snapdeal has had to wriggle out of the clutches of investors, one can comment positively on such tenaciousness.[10]

Born to a grain merchant, Bansal completed his bachelor's degree in engineering from IIT Delhi, and Bahl earned a dual bachelor's degree in marketing and operations strategy and manufacturing engineering from the Wharton School and

---

[9] Munira Rangwala, 'Tech Startups Have a Notoriously High Failure Rate, and Here's Possibly Why', Yourstory.com, 10 November 2017, https://yourstory.com/2017/11/why-tech-start-ups-fail/

[10] Aman Malik, 'Kunal Bahl: Entrepreneur Who Thrives on Failures', 7 August 2017, https://www.vccircle.com/kunal-bahl-the-entrepreneur-who-thrives-on-failures/

the School of Engineering and Applied Science, University of Pennsylvania.[11]

Bahl also completed an executive marketing programme from Kellogg School of Management. Ever the dreaming entrepreneur, studying in the US, Bahl started a detergent company and worked to sell his product at Walmart stores. He worked with Microsoft for a short period and returned to India in 2008. This, of course, turned out to be a blessing in disguise, as this was when he met his old school friend Bansal and began working on a plan for the creation of Snapdeal.

The company, like all others, prided itself in its culture, which, for the most part, contributed to its initial success. The values are mentioned below.[12]

- Innovation: freedom to take responsible risks
- Change: to evolve
- Openness: sharing ideas and feedback
- Ownership: collaboration with individual accountability
- Honesty: doing the right thing

The core-value campaign was undertaken by Snapdeal—'Dil ki Deal', with actor Aamir Khan as its brand ambassador—and speaking at length about the company's values, Bahl and Bansal launched the campaign with a vision to create India's most impactful digital commerce ecosystem that creates life-changing experiences for all its buyers and sellers alike.

In February 2010, when Bahl and Bansal decided that they wanted to start their own business, they chose an offline couponing

---

[11] Aarti Mahendru, 'Snapdeal Success Story: From Offline Coupon Business to Consumer-Focused Technology Company', http://www.cbsmohali.org/img/Dr.%20Aartil%20case%20study.pdf

[12] Startupstories.in, https://www.startupstories.in/stories/inspirational-stories/snapdeal-success-story-founders-kunal-bahl-and-rohit-bansal-biography

or a daily-deals platform and aptly named it MoneySaver. Within three months, 15,000 coupons had been sold. Bahl and Bansal thought it was time to take the company to the next level.

It was at this time that they met Vani Kola, a venture capitalist and one of Fortune India's most powerful women in Indian business. An idea lover and a former Silicon Valley entrepreneur, Kola is founder and managing director of Kalaari Capital, a firm with an impressive portfolio of clients, the likes of Urban Ladder, Zivame and POPxo. She has been awarded the 2015 Economic Times Midas Touch Award for her legendary trendspotting capabilities. She works with first-time entrepreneurs to build strong global technology companies. She leverages India's domestic growth to create high-growth enterprises.

Kola was initially unimpressed with what Bahl and Bansal had to offer. But after a couple of turbulent meetings, she started to warm up to the idea, and Kalaari Capital finally decided to invest in Bahl and Bansal. Snapdeal finally went online in 2010. The first few months, as with most tech start-ups, was a bumpy ride. Some hard mistakes were made and tough lessons learnt.

Of course, Snapdeal's climb to success was all but easy. The reason the company reached the heights it did was because it followed one simple policy: offering the best to its customers.

Hard work and perseverance to give its customers the very best and simple, straightforward core values gave Snapdeal its initial success. In November 2011, inspired by the success of Alibaba, Bahl and Bansal shut down the daily-deals platform and created an online marketplace. The move came as a surprise to its investors, as it had 70 per cent share of the daily-deals business. It was a make-or-break decision. In that moment, tech giant eBay was the only marketplace in India. Bahl was, however, able to convince the board and explained that the decision made much more sense in the long run for the continuing success of Snapdeal. The present form of Snapdeal soon started to take shape.[13]

---

[13] M. Mohanraj and M. Sakthivel, *Customer Perception about Online Shopping*, Tamilnadu: Edupedia Publications, 2017.

In August 2015, Bahl vehemently claimed in an interview with an Indian newspaper that his Snapdeal would topple arch-rival Flipkart, which was perched at the top of the Indian e-commerce market. He gave Snapdeal seven months to do so.

'The one thing I am very, very clear about right now is that I think we're going to be No. 1 [in terms of sales] by March 2016. I think we're going to beat Flipkart by then,' Bahl said in an interview with *Economic Times*. 'I'm very confident that whatever their [Flipkart's] numbers are, we will be ahead of them by March [2016].'[14]

Snapdeal did go on to become one of the largest online marketplaces in India, offering an assortment of 10 million products across diverse categories from over 100,000 sellers, shipping to more than 5,000 towns and cities in India. In March 2015, Snapdeal brought actor Aamir Khan for the promotion of its website in India.[15]

Snapdeal has received several rounds of funding. It received its first funding worth $12 million from Nexus Venture Partners and Indo-US Venture Partners in January 2011. This was followed by another round in July 2011 worth $45 million from Bessemer Venture Partners and existing investors. The third round of funding was worth $50 million and came from eBay and other pre-existing investors.

Three years later, in February 2014, Snapdeal raised funding of $133 million. This round was led by eBay, with participation from the institutional investors then: Kalaari Capital, Nexus Venture Partners, Bessemer Venture Partners, Intel Capital and Saama Capital. In May of the same year, funding worth $105 million

---

[14] Anirban Sen and Mihir Dalal, 'Snapdeal: Rise and fall of an Indian unicorn', LiveMint, 28 April 2017, https://www.livemint.com/Companies/8bzgpgNg8jeDM22YVydk5I/Snapdeal-Rise-and-fall-of-an-Indian-unicorn.html

[15] Shrutika Verma and Vidhi Choudhary, 'Snapdeal hires Aamir Khan as its brand ambassador', LiveMint, 18 March 2015, https://www.livemint.com/Companies/LWNWJijLzyjGTyHniZ49xN/Snapdeal-hires-Aamir-Khan-as-its-brand-ambassador.html

was raised. This was backed by investors BlackRock, Temasek Holdings, Premjiinvest and others. SoftBank invested $647 million in October 2014, making it the largest investor in Snapdeal so far.

In August 2015, Alibaba Group, Foxconn and SoftBank invested $500 million as fresh capital. In February the following year, one of the world's largest pension funds, Ontario Teachers' Pension Plan, and Singapore-based investment entity Brother Fortune Apparel led an investment worth $200 million in the Jasper Infotech-owned company. In May 2017, Snapdeal raised funding worth Rs 113 crore from Nexus Venture Partners.[16]

Once Snapdeal gained momentum, it didn't look back. Bahl and Bansal went on an acquisition spree—in June 2011, buying Bengaluru-based group-buying site Grabbon; in April 2012, Delhi-based online sports-goods retailer Esportsbuy.com, quickly followed by Shopo.in, an online marketplace for Indian handicraft products; and then, in April 2014, fashion products discovery site Doozton.com was acquired. Gift recommendation site Giftpicker was acquired in December of that same year.

This wasn't the end, however. In January 2015, it acquired a stake in product-comparison website Smartprix.com, followed by the acquisition of luxury fashion products discovery site Exclusively.in. In March, the firm acquired a 20 per cent stake in logistics service company Gojavas.com. Two more acquisitions in the same month were e-commerce management software and fulfilment solution provider Unicommerce.com and RupeePower, a digital platform for financial transactions. In April 2015, mobile-payments company FreeCharge.com was acquired. Programmatic display advertising platform Reduce Data was acquired in September of the same year. In August 2016, logistics

---

[16] Anirban Sen and Mihir Dalal, 'Snapdeal: Rise and Fall of an Indian Unicorn', LiveMint, 28 April 2017, https://www.livemint.com/Companies/8bzgpgNg8jeDM22YVydk5I/Snapdeal-Rise-and-fall-of-an-Indian-unicorn.html

firm Pigeon Express acquired a 51 per cent stake in GoJavas, with Snapdeal holding a 49 per cent stake in the firm.[17]

The following table takes a consolidated look at Snapdeal's acquisitions:

Reduce Data	September 2015
Shopo (Relaunched at App)	July 2015
Letgomo Labs	June 2015
Mart Mobi	May 2015
Freecharge	April 2015
Rupee Power	March 2015
Exclusively	February 2015
Wishpicker	December 2014
Doozton	April 2014
eSportsbuy	April 2012
Grabbon	June 2010

Snapdeal's acquisition of Freecharge was the biggest in the history of digital India at the time.

In August 2016, whispers began in the online community through a VCC exclusive article that Snapdeal was considering possibilities of a merger with its bigger rivals, Flipkart and Amazon. The speculations became more concrete in April 2017, when media houses reported that SoftBank, one of the major investors in Snapdeal, wanted the company to merge with Flipkart. Discussions on a merger with Flipkart went on for several months and ended in July 2017, when the deal failed to get the approval of all the investors, as required by the terms put forth by Flipkart.

---

[17] 'Pigeon Express in Talks to Buy Out Snapdeal's GoJavas Stake', LiveMint, 16 March 2017, https://www.livemint.com/Companies/Ua2ult2aTB5cWOI5HJqhbK/Pigeon-Express-in-talks-to-buy-out-Snapdeals-GoJavas-stake.html

The reasons for Snapdeal's downturn were many. No proper differentiation, poor acquisitions and cash burn in building too many warehouses were some of the reasons.

But the one that stands out the most is its omni-channel strategy. When it was launched in October 2015, many experts saw it as a possible game changer for Snapdeal. Organized retail in the country itself was becoming increasingly omni-channel, with conglomerates like Tata (with TataCLiQ) hopping on to the e-commerce bandwagon. It had been promised that customers could discover products online and order with faster hyperlocal fulfilment executed by offline retailers.

It also let users access value-added services, including demonstration, installation, activation or returns, at a store near them. Importantly, with this, the customer was able to procure products within two hours of ordering and access these services at the nearest store if they chose the pick-up option across seventy cities in India.

This model had great potential—with initial tie-ups with Mobile Store, Shoppers Stop, etc. With efficient implementation, it could have given Snapdeal a turnaround, but failed to make waves due to strategic mismanagement.

A former senior executive at Snapdeal once said that the omni-channel team had faced chaos from within. 'The leadership team had little power. They were unable to resource it to culmination because it needed a dedicated tech team of engineers which it was not provided with,' the executive said.[18]

In the Indian e-commerce sector's consolidation, Snapdeal's merger with Flipkart would have been the first big event to lead the way. In fact, this acquisition could have given a fresh lease of life to Snapdeal. After all, Jabong gained positive unit economics after it was acquired by the Flipkart–Myntra alliance. The founders (and existing investor Nexus Venture Partners) pouring in Rs 113 crore

---

[18]   Athira Nair, 'Seven Sins of Snapdeal: How and Where They Lost Their Way', Yourstory.com, 30 May 2017, https://yourstory.com/2017/05/snapdeal-sins?utm_pageloadtype=scroll

in a surprise move also showed that the stakeholders had not lost all hope yet.

Both Bansal and Bahl, however, opposed the merger strongly. There were several causes for the merger deal to fall apart and this was followed by the founders taking a decision to continue operating Snapdeal as an independent company, and thus began the vision of Snapdeal 2.0. Even as this decision was being made, Snapdeal sold Freecharge to Axis Bank for Rs 385 crore, almost 90 per cent less than what it paid for the firm in 2015.[19]

The turbulent journey of Snapdeal culminated in the founders, Bahl and Bansal, sending an email to all the employees of the company. In it, they mentioned that the fate of their company was no longer in their hands and that the investors were 'driving the discussions around the way forward'. The email came as a surprise to many and was considered a kind of 'confession' of the mistakes made by the founders, which had led them to their current predicament.

As reported by *MintAsia*, this was how the email went: 'There has been a lot of media reporting and speculation around Snapdeal recently. While our investors are driving the discussions around the way forward, I am reaching out to let you know that the well-being of the entire team is my and Rohit's top and only priority. We will do all that we can, and more, in working with our investors to ensure that there is no disruption in employment and that there are positive professional as well as financial outcomes for the team as the way forward becomes clear.'

The email was sent with the intention of boosting employee morale after large-scale lay-offs, falling monthly sales and shutdowns of under-performing units plagued the journey of Snapdeal.

---

[19] 'Snapdeal sells Freecharge at 90% discount to Axis Bank', *Economic Times*, 27 July 2017, https://retail.economictimes.indiatimes.com/news/e-commerce/e-tailing/snapdeal-sells-freecharge-at-90-discount-to-axis-bank/59792247

Despite having a rough couple of years, Snapdeal was far from ready to throw in the towel. In the beginning of 2018 and as the strategy for Snapdeal 2.0 slowly began to take shape, the company started to 'trim the fat', so to speak. Future Supply Chain Solutions said that it would acquire Snapdeal's logistics service provider, Vulcan Express Pvt Ltd, in an all-cash deal of around Rs 35 crore. Jason Kothari, chief strategy and investment officer at Snapdeal, mentioned that this move would be beneficial to all three parties, much like the recent Freecharge sale. He said, 'Snapdeal divests off an asset that is non-strategic in nature for Snapdeal 2.0, allowing it to focus its capital and management on its core e-commerce business. According to him, this move allows the company to focus on its core e-commerce business.'[20]

In May, an Ahmedabad-based e-commerce firm, Infibeam, said that it would be buying Unicommerce eSolutions, a warehouse management firm from Snapdeal, for Rs 120 crore, in a non-cash deal, in continuation with its 'focus on one core e-commerce business' strategy.

As part of this strategy, the co-founders, who, as of 2018, together owned a 6.5 per cent stake in Snapdeal, decided to lead the company into a 'new and compelling' direction by selling the non-core assets. What do these moves signify for the e-commerce giant? Even though the founders and top executives are certain that the decision to sell auxiliary businesses to pave the way for the future of the core business was a sound one, analysts are not too sure about it. According to Yugal Joshi, a start-up analyst at Everest Group, Snapdeal is cutting out businesses that are essential for an e-commerce business to flourish. Another independent consultant, Harish HV, argues that with all the selling of non-core businesses, Snapdeal is trying to stay afloat and realize whatever value they can. He also goes on to explain that

---

[20] Anirban Ghoshal, 'Future Group Acquires Snapdeal's Logistics Arm Vulcan Express for $5.5 mn', Vccircle.com, 27 January 2018, https://www.vccircle.com/future-group-acquires-snapdeals-logistics-arm-vulcan-express-for-5-5-mn/

Snapdeal is holding a heavy marketing silence. The absence of TV advertising and promotions is jarring, and any other push towards an increase in sales seems to be non-existent.

Whatever may be the decisions Snapdeal takes in the future, it doesn't look like the end of the road for Snapdeal just yet. The tenacity of the founders has been tested and they are profitable today. That gives them time to lick their wounds and stay focused on the business. We hope that they can continue making a profit and morph when the time comes and the opportunity presents itself, as it inevitably will.

4. Naukri.com: Bikhchandani's Single-Minded Focus

As the old adage says, an organization's most valuable resource is its people, more specifically its youth. History and common sense both dictate that the development of a country's youth should be treated as a long-term investment. This policy on a smaller scale should be followed by organizations at large. But sadly, this isn't the case. In fact, reality is far from it.

The problem is that many organizations see training as an expense and not an investment. This ignorance on the part of organizations, of course, costs a lot as the employees soon update their résumés and LinkedIn profiles and start the extensive process of job hunting. And we are now in an age where job hunting happens in the comfort of our own homes or from the very same offices employees want to escape.[21]

The business of online job hunting has taken the world by storm ever since the late nineties. A job portal is a website that deals with employment and careers. An applicant can submit their résumé, update an online profile and get job advertisements directly emailed to them. Nowadays, employment websites even offer career and

---

[21] 'The True Cost of Not Providing Employee Training', Shift Learning, 19 April 2018, https://www.shiftelearning.com/blog/the-true-cost-of-not-providing-employee-training

job-search advice. There are people who will even help you redo your entire CV and social media presence to better your chances of employment.

In India, the trend of online job search continues to grow, with the youth becoming more and more active online. With the advent of smartphones, the seemingly never-ending search for the perfect job has become all the more easier and accessible.

Naukri.com was one of the earliest sites launched in India and also one of the biggest. Let us look at its story in detail.

Info Edge, the parent company of Naukri.com, was launched on 1 May 1995. It is now one of the premier Internet-based businesses in India. It primarily provides online classifieds services. Over a period of almost two decades, it has steadily developed a portfolio of brands across different domains. This all began when Sanjeev Bikhchandani, the founder of Info Edge, left his cushy corporate job at Glaxo Consumer Products (then Hindustan Milkfood Manufacturers) and founded two companies, Info Edge and Indmark. Info Edge worked on salary reports for college graduates such as engineers and MBAs. Each salary report was sold to companies for a sum of anywhere between Rs 5000 to 10,000.

Some problems made both the partners of Info Edge and Indmark part ways. Sanjeev was left with Info Edge and his partner took Indmark. During a visit to an IT fair at Delhi's Pragati Maidan, Sanjeev attended some workshops on how the Internet exactly worked. The Internet was still in its nascent stages in India in the nineties, and with the help of his brother Sushil in the US, Sanjeev hired a server, with a monthly rent of about $25. The brothers then mutually decided that Sushil will have a 5 per cent share in Info Edge.

In the beginning, things didn't look so rosy for Sanjeev and his company. The recession hit in 1996 and the company was suffering losses. He then confided in a friend, Anil Lall, who was a software programmer at the time and later the chief technical officer at Naukri.com; they both hit upon the idea of naukri.com.

Naukri was launched on 2 April 1997, and the first version of the website had over 1000 jobs collected from twenty-nine newspapers. Many things happened simultaneously after that. Business magazines started posting reviews about the site, word-of-mouth marketing and a lot of articles in newspapers about the site led to a slow and steady increase in traffic.[22]

A graduate in economics from St Stephen's College, Delhi, and an alumnus of IIM Ahmedabad, Sanjeev Bikhchandani always dreamt of starting something of his own. During his brief stint at Glaxo Consumer, he realized that people were always talking about moving on in their careers or changing jobs or just looking for what's 'out there'. Sanjeev realized that jobs were an extremely high-interest category and that headhunting had tremendous potential, especially in a growing economy like India.

What started out as a partnership in 1989, slowly moved on and became a highly fragmented database of jobs by the early nineties. Sanjeev and his partners worked out of the servant's quarters above the garage in his father's house and paid him a rent of Rs 800 per month. In the initial months, it was salary surveys and other databases. Sanjeev had to keep his day job and worked for the *Pioneer* alongside his stint with Naukri.

The site started getting profitable from the second year onwards. The revenue climbed to a cool Rs 1.2 million from Rs 2,00,000 in the second year. He made do with his own financials until the year 2000. He then received some funding from ICICI Venture Capital. As many would like to, they have only used one round of funding, of about Rs 73 million.[23]

During the initial months at Naukri, around March 1997, only a handful of Indians were online. There were other hurdles as well.

---

[22] Sangeeta Singh, 'How I made My 1st Million: Naukri.com CEO', Rediff. com, 23 July 2005, https://www.rediff.com/money/2005/jul/23spec2.htm
[23] Rajshree Kukreti, 'Hire and Higher', *Business Today*, 2 November 2006, https://www.businesstoday.in/moneytoday/new-business/hire-and-higher/story/6255.html

The founders were not familiar with venture capital or dot-com valuations. They just felt that this would be a good idea and ran with it. Sanjeev began to directly approach HR managers via direct mail and tell them about job listings.

These listings were free at the time and revenue was obviously sluggish, but slowly and surely traffic to the career website soared. At that point in time, parent company Info Edge abandoned all other projects and put all its resources in Naukri.

Within the next two years, the Internet had taken India by storm. Naukri's turnover had almost doubled, to Rs 3.6 million, and venture capitalists started knocking on their doors. Sanjeev sold 15 per cent of Info Edge to ICICI Prudential Technology Fund for Rs 7.29 crores in April 2000. His reasoning was that ICICI had greater 'investor compatibility'.

New office premises were acquired but Naukri had a very frugal nature. Sanjeev was modest, almost to a fault, and had an agenda of not spending too much on advertising.

In 2006, however, Naukri released a slew of TV ads about an arrogant boss called Hari Sadu. He was a work of fiction—a caricature of a demanding and evil boss. The message behind the ad was that every employee had options; that they didn't have to work under tyrants like Hari Sadu when Naukri.com was around. The ad created waves as countless employees related to the subordinates depicted in it. Employees felt that someone had their backs while they dealt with their own Hari Sadus; that things weren't dire and that in most times, they could just look for another job.[24]

Naukri's business model was divided into two: B2B and B2C. They provided end-to-end recruitment assistance to companies

---

[24] Nikhil Mehta and Upasna Agrwal, 'Hari Sadu Versus Subordinates: An Analysis of the Interpersonal Dynamics at the Workplace', *IUP Journal of Soft Skills*, January 2017, https://www.researchgate.net/publication/317032370_ Hari_Sadu_Versus_Subordinates_An_Analysis_of_the_Interpersonal_ Dynamics_at_the_Workplace

from small clients to big-ticket firms. Apart from the usual, résumé databases, vacancy listing, etc., they also provided email and text marketing. For customers, they provided résumé writing, profile enhancement and recruiter reach services. Hence their marketing strategies always had to be two-fold in nature.

Organic traffic made up for most eyeballs on Naukri.com, but strategies such as search engine marketing and optimization also contributed to this. Post 2010, new social media platforms such as Twitter, Facebook and LinkedIn have also influenced Naukri's reach to customers.[25]

Over the years Naukri has bagged several awards. A list of these accolades is mentioned below:

2006 – Received the Consumer Connect 'Campaign of the Year' award for the Hari Sadu commercial at the Advertising Club, Kolkata.

2006 – Received the 'Red Herring Asia 100' 2006 award for the INSTA HIRE Solution.

2007 – Won the 'Best TVC India and South Asia' at the CASBAA (Cable and Satellite Broadcasting Association of Asia) TV Advertising Awards for the Hari Sadu 'Name Calling' commercial.

2012 – Recognized as the best classified website at the second edition of the India Digital Awards, organized by the Internet and Mobile Association of India (IAMAI).

2014 – Received Metrixlab's Best Website of the Year (WOTY) award in the career and education segment.

As India grows at the rate of 7 per cent a year, the job market seems to remain stagnant. Many of our youth have been struggling

---

[25] 'Case Study: How Naukri.com Became #No1 Indian Job Portal When the Internet Was in Its Infancy' Delhi School of Internet Marketing, 30 October 2015, https://dsim.in/blog/2015/10/30/case-studyhow-naukri-com-became-no1-indian-job-portal-when-the-internet-was-in-its-infancy/

to find jobs that match their qualifications since the economic crisis of 2008. This bleak picture has improved to a certain extent, though. There has been a steady rise in campus recruitment drives and lateral hires across sectors as well. There has been a quantum increase in job offers, salary levels and diversity of recruiters/pre-placement offers too.[26]

What does this spell out for Naukri and how are they tapping this potential market of new job seekers and graduates every year? Although government data on the job market is a little patchy, with workplaces becoming more and more dynamic—for example many companies now welcome back new mothers to work, there is a work-from-home option being increasingly made available in the market for job seekers and so on—there is not a lack of options. With the launch of Firstnaukri.com, fresh graduates get a slew of services that the company offers. An in-depth understanding of the market, career guidance and CV writing, to name a few of the numerous services offered in an effort to make entry-level hiring easier for recruiters and job seekers alike.

The Future of Online Talent Acquisition

With the increase in artificial intelligence and machine learning, Naukri is now looking at personalization in various processes to cater to the needs of both the recruiter and job seeker. An example of this increase in automation was shared by V. Suresh, chief sales officer at Naukri: job application rankings determined by learning-based match scores, real-time job recommendations to job seekers based on their profiles, etc., are some of the areas.

---

[26] Malini Goyal, 'India's Job Market Set to Turn the Corner in 2018 as Campus Placements Show Spurt', *Economic Times*, 10 December, 2017, https://economictimes.indiatimes.com/jobs/indias-job-market-set-to-turn-the-corner-in-2018-as-campus-placements-show-spurt/articleshow/62001845.cms?from=mdr

He further went on to state that at Naukri, enhancing the interactions between recruiters and job seekers, was always on the agenda. With the introduction of mobile apps, all recruitment workflows were likely to become more and more invested in the job board, and hence Naukri was looking to scale up with innovative solutions on both web and mobile platforms.[27]

With India becoming a star market for the rest of the world, and the Indian economy itself growing the way it has, Naukri as well as other job boards only have good things to look forward to in the future. How they make use of this remains to be seen. However, this market surely has begun to show early signs of fatigue as it stands today.

5. Bharatmatrimony.com: Janakiraman Arranges Marriages

Naru writes, 'Murugavel Janakiraman has the youthful looks of a thirty-two-year-old start-up entrepreneur. He was an early member of the Chennai Angels and TiE Chennai, and my contact with him was somewhat limited. Sometime later, and when I was the president of TiE Chennai, I had occasion to hold a press conference to bring to everyone's attention the unfair treatment meted out to a start-up founder. At the time, Janakiraman's company had gone bust, and his inability to pay off his debts landed him in a soup and in jail for "cheating". As president of TiE, I felt obliged to highlight this to the political leaders around the world that this was unfair and trumped up. I also believed that incidents of this kind were detrimental to the business community, more specifically the start-up community. When I arrived at the press conference venue, who did I see sitting in the front row? None other than Janakiraman himself. A reassuring

---

[27] Amol Pawar, 'Recruitment Workflows Are Likely to Move Online across Sectors: V. Suresh, Naukri.com', PeopleMatters.in, 26 June 2018, https://www.peoplematters.in/article/hiring/recruitment-workflows-are-likely-to-move-online-across-sectors-v-suresh-naukricom-18616

smile on his face, his presence added greater value to the press conference and boosted my own morale.'

When one thinks of India, what comes to mind? Our diversity? The largest democracy in the world? Our culture and heritage? Our ancient traditions? Yoga? So many things come to mind when we think of our country.

One tradition that has been a part of Indian culture is arranged marriage. What is an arranged marriage? Arranged marriage is a type of union where the bride and groom are selected by individuals other than the bride and groom themselves, most often by their families or relatives. Arranged marriages are an inherent part of Indian culture and still account for a majority of marriages in India.[28]

However, since marriages between people of mixed cultural backgrounds are becoming the new norm in the cities and are also being portrayed on screen by the Hindi film industry, arranged marriages too have appropriately adapted to the changing landscape of Indian society. A more modernized outlook of the families of young brides and grooms, resulting in the rise of 'self-arranged' marriages and nuclear families, has given a new definition to the entire idea of an arranged marriage.

Along with this new form of 'arranged' marriage, the techniques of scouting for prospective brides and grooms have also evolved, leading to the rise of online matrimonial services in India. These services have been around for fifteen years now. The role of the matchmaker or mediator has always been very important in arranged marriages and this has been passed on from elderly relatives and well-connected friends to brokers and pundits and then to newspaper ads, finally paving the way for the

---

[28] Kavita Das, 'India Has Changed a Lot in 70 Years. But Arranged Marriage Remains the Norm', *Washington Post*, 2 May 2017, https://www. washingtonpost.com/news/soloish/wp/2017/05/02/india-has-changed-a-lot-in-70-years-but-arranged-marriage-remains-the-norm/

matrimonial website. This was an unorganized aspect of life in India, a fruit ripe for the picking and to build further on, and that is exactly what this venture is about.

Online portals and matrimonial websites became the welcome and trusted sources of information without the hassle of human error and dealing with relatives. And with this began the era of online matrimonial websites. They cater to everything from greetings to meetings, from success stories to event management, and they capture it all so beautifully on their websites. There may be plenty of these sites out there, Vivah.com, Jeevansathi.com, Shaadi.com to name a few, but the one that started it all was Bharatmatrimony.com, and this is its story.

The son of a labourer, Murugavel Janakiraman, grew up in an industrial suburb in the northern part of the city of Chennai. He had little to no exposure to the world of academia. In an interview with the *Economic Times,* he says, 'Our house was one of a row in the alleys of Royapuram. My father was a labourer and there weren't many in the family or in the neighbourhood to look to for advice when it came to pursuing academic interests.'[29]

As he grew up, he chose to obtain his undergraduate degree in Chemistry. This was because he was convinced that this would help him secure a job as a lab technician and that, according to him, would be his greatest achievement. But his scores in mathematics and statistics led him on the path of programming. A few jobs later, in the nineties, when Muruga, as he was called by family and friends, was working as a software consultant for Lucent Technologies in Edison, New Jersey, he set up a web portal and an information website for the Tamil community. Matrimony was only one of the

[29] Bharani Vaitheesvaran, 'I Am Married to and through Bharat Matrimony: Murugavel Janakiraman', *Economic Times*, 15 September 2017, https://economictimes.indiatimes.com/small-biz/entrepreneurship/i-am-married-to-and-through-bharat-matrimony-murugavel-janakiraman/articleshow/60525006.cms

website's numerous offerings. When Muruga realized that most of the traffic to the site was generated by the matrimonial section, he decided to branch off into a separate site dedicated solely to the business of arranged marriages, and this is how Bharat Matrimony was born.

Muruga started with a meagre investment of about $10 per month and within two years was able to invest $1000 per month. Matrimony.com raised Rs 100 crore in two rounds of funding and finally went public in September 2017.[30]

As Muruga started his journey to success, an event that could have been catastrophic actually worked in the company's favour. This was Y2K and the dot-com bust that closely followed a lot of people letting go of their online presence altogether. This in turn led to a lot of software employees losing their jobs and Muruga was one of them. But instead of looking for a new job, Muruga took this as a sign of things to come and decided to focus completely on Matrimony.com.[3]

At the time when the website was launched, the Internet was in its infancy in India. This decision to branch out to a separate matrimonial website did pay off well for him literally as well as figuratively, as he realized that people were willing to pay for these services online or at least were beginning to look at this as a viable option as compared to the newspaper ads and pundits that were still largely responsible for the business of matchmaking. It was still just the early noughties after all, and he wanted to provide easy access and payment options to everyone. So much so that the company decided to embark upon and pioneered 'doorstep collections'. As made evident in the name itself, this was a precursor to 'Cash on Delivery', which made things a whole lot easier for the company.

Bharat Matrimony was more than just a means to make a living for Muruga. In 1999, the matchmaking platform helped him find his

---

[30] Ibid.

own wife. In his own words, he is 'married to and married through' Bharat Matrimony.[31]

After the introduction of 'doorstep collections' in 2000, to further expand their operations to the customers who were not Internet savvy, Bharat Matrimony launched retail outlets in 2001, with the first one at Adyar Chennai. It now has 139 company-owned outlets.

The following year, Bharat Matrimony hosted the largest matrimony meet in the world. 'Mega Swayamvaram 2002', conducted at Rajah Muthiah and Rani Meyammai Halls in Chennai, was a matrimony meet concept through which prospective brides and grooms and their families could meet face to face. The event had an online-registration model which helped increase footfall to the event and made it a grand success.

Following the success of this mega event, Muruga and Bharat Matrimony reached out to all kinds of audiences (members and non-members) including members who were differently abled and had special needs. The event, held in Mumbai and Delhi, drew a large crowd of over a thousand people and was the first of its kind ever. It led to an overwhelming response from people with special needs and provided a certain comfort level and platform for people to interact with each other.

The road ahead was steep for Muruga. He now had to keep up with several competitors making their presence felt. Not only that, the customers who were interested in getting married in their own community were finding it difficult with the increasing number of registrations on the site. Muruga gave this some thought and came up with the solution of segmenting the platform into various sites depending on community. Soon, fifteen regional domains were launched—TamilMatrimony, TeluguMatrimony, BengalMatrimony, HindiMatrimony and plenty more. All this

---

[31] Ibid.

from a 300-square-foot office in the heart of the busy bylanes of Thyagaraya Nagar in Chennai.[32]

The coming years looked promising for the wedding giant as global players Yahoo and Canaan Partners invested a cool $8.65 million in the Bharat Matrimony Group. Apart from the launch of its regional sites, Muruga was looking to expand in other areas of the lucrative business of marriage as well, with MatrimonyPhotography and MatrimonyMandap to name a few. Another area that Muruga thought could be tapped was the Indian elite. Globalization and liberalization contributed to the proliferation of the rich and affluent in India, and EliteMatrimony was launched to cater to their niche matchmaking requirements. At this point in time Muruga and BharatMatrimony got another feather in their caps, with an entry in the Limca Book of Records for a record number of marriages online.[33]

In 2008, with the economic crisis looming large over the world economy and the increasing number of pink slip handouts and pay cuts, the matrimony market not only took a downturn, but the needs of the customers shifted course in India towards the public sector, which is usually associated with stability. NRI grooms, who were in strong demand especially in the southern states of Tamil Nadu and Andhra Pradesh, were now not looking as appealing as before. Brides and their families were now looking towards grooms with jobs in the public sector. There was also a shift in the women's criteria for prospective grooms. With jobs of their own, financial stability and more independence, many Indian women did not want to move abroad after getting married.

---

[32] 'Divide And Rule', Magzter, https://www.magzter.com/article/Business/Outlook-Business/Divide-And-Rule.

[33] Anupama Chandrasekaran, 'Bharatmatrimony.com Owner Consim Postpones Public Issue.' LiveMint, 13 August 2009, https://www.livemint.com/Companies/w5kvWekzFLdLbktT6s06aK/Bharatmatrimonycom-owner-Consim-postpones-public-issue.html.

The global financial meltdown also led to a cash burn of about Rs 2 crore per month, and Muruga had less than half a year to control the problem. Muruga decided to handle only product development and technology. Apart from this, a lot of microsites were shut down overnight and some people were let go.

Muruga's perseverance is the one quality that stands out as described by Vishal Gupta, MD, Bessemer Venture Partners. He also talks about Muruga's frugality—being able to build a successful company without spending millions of dollars was his biggest success.

In its twenty-year existence, as of 2018, Bharat Matrimony has been able to raise a total of $ 20.4 million over two rounds of funding, the last being on 5 February 2008. And as mentioned before, with the previous investments from Yahoo and Canaan Partners, Bharat Matrimony raised $8.65 million and was well on its way to success.

In 2008, it earned the winning position at the Deloitte Technology Fast 50 India programme. This was conducted every year by Deloitte Touche Tohmatsu, Asia-Pacific. In another round of funding, Consim Info raised another $11.75 million through Mayfield Fund and other existing investors.

In fact, in the years that followed, Bharat Matrimony and Murugavel earned plenty of accolades. It holds multiple world records for the largest wedding album, and on 27 May, during an online matrimony meet, the company conducted hundred meets in one day for different communities. During the three-hour meet, members could chat, exchange views and share horoscopes with other members of their community. Participation in the event was excellent.

Murugavel had always been fine-tuned to the needs of the consumer from the very beginning. He understood that making Bharat Matrimony more mobile-friendly was the future and in 2011 launched apps for all their major platforms. As of 2018, the company has a staggering 7 million downloads, including regional and community apps.

Murugavel had been nominated twice by the *Economic Times* as 'Entrepreneur of the Year' and was also awarded the 'Digital Entrepreneur of the Year' award by WAT. In 2013, he was also the chairman of the IAMAI or the Internet and Mobile Association of India.[34]

The company was ranked as India's most trusted matrimony brand in the trust report of 2014 in a survey conducted across sixteen cities throughout India. The survey covers over 20,000 brands and is conducted by Trust Research Advisory (TRA) annually.

MiMA, short for Matrimony.com's Intelligent Matchmaking Algorithm, won the prestigious NASSCOM award for Top 50 Excellence in Analytics in the year 2015.

With these numerous feathers in its cap, the company, with Murugavel at the helm, only looked ahead now to tap the unlimited potential of the $56 billion marital services industry. With this thought process, the company forayed into many services such as MatrimonyPhotography and videography, and MatrimonyBazaar for services ranging from clothing to catering, and MatrimonyMandaps to help customers find venues for their weddings.

In 2017, the company was the first to be listed in the stock exchange as a pure play consumer Internet company.[35]

As it rapidly expands its global presence, the company has not forgotten that the Indian market will always be its biggest source of growth. With one of the largest workforces in the world and a high percentage of them within the 'marriageable age' and only a percentage of this online, Murugavel plans to increase membership and expand its user base. He has always operated with a customer-

---

[34] 'Speakers: the Talk', Thetalk.in, http://www.thetalk.in/big-ideas-to-scale-sme-startups.php.

[35] Bharani Vaitheesvaran, 'I Am Married to and through Bharat Matrimony: Murugavel Janakiraman', *Economic Times*, September 15, 2017, https://economictimes.indiatimes.com/small-biz/entrepreneurship/i-am-married-to-and-through-bharat-matrimony-murugavel-janakiraman/articleshow/60525006.cms

centric philosophy, and as they move forward, customers will continue to be their main focus. The services they provide are very personal and the experience is very different for every individual; this means that going the extra mile to help customers find their dream life partner and have a dream wedding goes a long way.[36]

Murugavel and the company believe in the 3Cs: Commitment, Competence and Continuous Learning. He believes in the power of technology in influencing our lives and in its ability to make something as stressful as finding a suitable life partner, and the ceremonies and events that follow, an easy and enjoyable experience. It is guesstimated that of the 60 million people looking for a spouse, only 10 per cent are online; how Murugavel and Bharat Matrimony tap this potential remains to be seen.

6. Thousand Sri Cities: Ravi Sannareddy

Fifty-five km north of Chennai, on the border of Tamil Nadu and Andhra Pradesh, lies Sri City.

Ravindra Sannareddy is the founder and managing director of Sri City. A native of Satyavedu Mandal, Ravi was born in 1964 in Aravapalem village, Andhra Pradesh, and schooled at the Panchayati Elementary School and Zilla Parishad High School. He went on to the Government College, Sullurupeta, for his undergraduate studies.

Sannareddy went on to complete his master's in water resources management and then did his PhD in environmental sciences from Johns Hopkins University, USA. This educational background and the early impressions of his youth gave him the resolve to make a long-lasting impact on society.

---

[36] 'BharatMatrimony's "Find Your Equal" Advertisement Starring MS Dhoni Drives Social Change', *Siasat Daily*, 19 December 2018, https://www.siasat.com/news/bharatmatrimonys-find-your-equal-advertisement-starring-ms-dhoni-drives-social-change-1447519/

Sannareddy had a vision and his vision has only expanded during the last twelve years as Sri City comes to life from a mere idea on a piece of paper. The conceptual paper was ambitious, designed to accommodate 500 industries, a total investment of over Rs 1,00,000 crore, with a potential to create 1,50,000 jobs in the region.

Sannareddy admits that while planning the start-up he never knew the challenges ahead of him. Nobody had built an industrial city from scratch, and bringing the grandiose plans to reality would prove more than a handful. And here he was, the son of an agriculturist, fully conversant with the utter poverty that existed around him in the district, and yet, with an ambitious masterplan that started off as an idea, striving to build something unique and different which would make an impact on the nation.

Sannareddy started drawing some boundaries around his idea. He wanted to be at the centre with Sriharikota to the east, Srikalahasti to the north; Sri Tirupati to the west and Sriperumbudur to the south. Each of these four cities had a 3000-plus-year history, with two of them having modern temples.

But you do think twice—and often subsequently—when you are about to embark on a voyage where even 'angels' fear to tread. The project was clearly just the kind that required a long gestation period, with far too many uncertainties that angel investors usually abhor. You can reasonably expect a surprise nearly every week and sometimes every day. When your entire investments are visibly etched on to a physical map of India, it's not long before you begin to see the problems. And they can come at a fairly high speed without any predictability of periodicity.

A politician once explained it to me during my entrepreneurial days, 'When you have so many visible and immovable assets out in the open, you have nowhere to run away. You will always negotiate.' But Ravindra Sannareddy was determined to achieve Keynesian full employment in the area where he was born. And his response to such veiled suggestions was to scale the operation visibly in a unique and citizen-friendly manner. Nobody in India had tried to build an industrial city of this size and magnitude. He considered himself fortunate to be able to contribute in this way to his birthplace. He was determined to win over the local population completely. Incidentally, we are at the halfway point today. The bulk of the 8000 acre property has been acquired and paid for. And there is no union anywhere in sight.

Villages within the campus have been left alone so that they can coexist. Sri City also generates its own solar electricity, shared by different areas in the city. Every week there is an invitation for Sannareddy from one state or the other, with a request to start a similar Sri City there. But such a plan is not on his mind.

Sannareddy is a son of the soil. His father is an agriculturist from the vicinity of Sri City and lives in Sullurupeta near Sriharikota, in Andhra Pradesh. His three daughters are working professionals and away.

To put together a management team that would virtually stay on campus called for very astute selection and some amount of luck. Sannareddy managed to find both when he roped in Ramesh Subramaniam, an ex-Tata employee, to accept the post of the CEO. Ramesh got into the act straight away and the results are staggering:

- Nearly 200 organizations are already located at Sri City.
- Over 50,000 from the vicinity are employed at Sri City.
- Sri City has over twenty-six Japanese companies already on campus.
- Only environment-friendly companies are permitted in Sri City.
- Three major academic institutions are already functioning on campus.
- No labour is available within a 40 km radius of the campus. The area has achieved full employment.
- Locals who had migrated to other parts of the country seeking employment have now started returning.
- A full-time HR centre is constantly training personnel to make them skill-ready for the industry.

- Over 50 per cent of those employed are women.
- One organization boasts a 100 per cent female workforce.

Every challenge has been converted into an opportunity. And that is the key to the success of Sri City. There are four main concepts around which Sri City thrives:

i.   *Sri City as a place of work*: Diverse and global culture has been brought to Sri City. Every day over 150 buses go into Chittoor district to transport workers to Sri City.
ii. *Sri City as a place to live*: Already, over 200 dwellings have been created, and more are under construction.
iii. *Sri City as a centre of learning*: Institute for Financial Management and Research (IFMR), Chinmaya school, Indian Institute of Information Technology (IIIT) and Krea University are already located here—and the search for more continues.
iv. *Sri City as a place to play*: Golf course provision, sports complex, multiplex are in the offing.

Sri City operates as a microcosm of how developing countries have operated. It is a forerunner in truly meeting the PM's goal of 'Made in India' and Andhra Pradesh's goal of 'Make in India'. India requires 100 Sri Cities across the nation. Only then can 15 million people be employed. And we would require this every year.

The business model here is somewhere between an infrastructure project and a real estate project. Land acquisition is a continuous business and a headache. As mentioned, Sannareddy receives constant requests, and usually from well-known and well-meaning friends, to meet up with dignitaries from other states in India who come to invite him to set up a similar unit in their state. These are politely declined by him, as they call for heavy time investment.

However, there are problems. For example, cash flow is a major issue. Sri City raised $25 million in June 2008. In October of the same year, Lehman Brothers went down; money became hard to come by. The $25 million raised barely sufficed and raising further funds became difficult and not easily viable. Cash flow was dependent on sale of land to new factories or institutions, so there was a constant cash drain on keeping existing assets intact and productive. Welcome to the real world!

Naru recalls his association with Sannareddy: 'I met Ravi Sannareddy when he was first introduced to the Chennai Angels as a new member. Prima facie, he does not at all come across as a successful businessman that he is, even though he wears his business tycoon hat. The reality is that I was intrigued to hear about the new industrial zone coming up on the border of Andhra Pradesh and Tamil Nadu. But when I heard that Chennai Business School and IFMR were both also shifting to Sri City, a mere curiosity became an obsession. Ravi was keen to hold one of our The Chennai Angels (TCA) meetings at Sri City, and using that as an excuse, I set off for Sri City. I fortified myself for a two-hour drive, but we got there in less than an hour and thirty minutes. And what a surprise it was for me! An immaculately laid out city had sprung up with a couple of hundred factories, and the most recent planned addition to Sri City family was Krea University. And of course, a fully functional Chinmaya school where disparate bunch of kids from various socio-economic backgrounds rubbed shoulders.'

Many of you may not have or have barely heard of Sri City. It does not market but instead follows a very unique strategy to sell themselves to individually selected companies.

There are three key characteristics that we observe in this entrepreneur:

1. A big vision
2. Humility and modesty
3. Delivering quality over mindless expansion

7. CAMS: Shankar and Long-Distance Running

This is what Naru recalls about his personal association with Vaidyanathan Shankar, the founder of Computer Age Management Services (CAMS), a technology-based financial infrastructure provider for mutual funds, VCFs, insurance companies: 'Shankar is an introvert and can often be mistaken for a very reserved person. We both hailed from the same alma mater, and I was present at an alumni function that felicitated Shankar with the Best Alumnus Award at IIMC. And, of course, it is no coincidence that he is also a member of The Chennai Angels (TCA). We are both members of the Madras Club and since we both stay a two-minute walk away from the club, we meet there every morning for a walk. Despite being an introvert, he has a fine sense of humour (he laughs at all my jokes!) and a fine mind that dissects any complex issue. Always a pleasure to talk to over a cup of coffee. Throw in a breakfast at the same venue, and Shankar can talk about his early days of entrepreneurship. When I heard of the feeble assistance that he got from his contemporaries during his struggling entrepreneurial years, I was reminded of my own struggle during my entrepreneurial days. I would, however, add that there is no bitterness whatsoever in him, and that he is always available to budding entrepreneurs for a quick mentoring session.'

Shankar is a good example of a well-qualified person attracted to becoming an entrepreneur. A graduate from IIT Madras and postgraduate from IIM Kolkata, Shankar pretty much represents the top end of the group that comprises highly qualified persons in the country. Lest you get intimidated by his qualifications, he is a quintessential south Indian who likes to keep things understated and his demeanour disarms you completely. It goes without saying that Shankar's personality is characterized by humility and modesty. Straight out of IIM, Shankar joined Pond's India in Chennai as a management trainee. After a core training programme, he was posted as a sales manager.

Shankar went into Pond's and worked in a variety of departments, including production. Shankar had studied entrepreneurship development programme (EDP) courses at the IIM, at a time when the punched-card system had barely been discontinued at the IIMs. India was just beginning to emerge as a possible contender for world recognition in the field of software development. After working for four years in Pond's, Shankar felt he was ready to shed the trappings of a multinational company and venture into the world of software development. At the time, the boom in software development was still just getting off the ground in India and Shankar was confident that he could write good code and quickly understand the clients' requirements.

Interestingly, Shankar, who was targeting the domestic market in India at the time, learnt that finding customers was very difficult. In summary, nobody wanted to pay for software, and customers were few and far between. It didn't take him long to figure out that this was going nowhere and that IT services in the domestic market were unlikely to lead to prosperity in the conceivable future. Shankar focused on manufacturing and trading verticals for his software development. Sparse furniture, a small office, a series of small but new jobs for development work, and constantly hunting for new business characterized the typical working day. The glamour of becoming an IT firm with a large cross section of engineers working for him seemed a far cry. In addition, his friends and contemporaries who worked for large Indian and multinational companies appeared to be prospering and living well. But as Shankar himself admitted, 'he had no expectations' and was focused on making good what he had started. Until somebody suggested that he should focus on the banking, financial services and insurance (BFSI) sector. And so Bombay as a market opened up and the real struggle began. The BFSI sector was in fact a fast-growing sector in the domestic market. It was also receiving the attention of all the IT services firms—small and big. Shankar estimates that there were over 150 firms competing in Mumbai in the BFSI sector.

Yet, by 1990, at the end of twelve years in business, CAMS had built a revenue of over Rs 10 crore in the IT business. In 1995, SEBI commenced the registration of firms as registrars in its move towards dematerializing storage of equity shares in repositories. CAMS was one of the early entrants. SEBI also mandated that when a new issue took place, the entire process of allocation, etc., needed to be completed within seventy days. It was clearly a task that was nearly physically impossible unless one either took shortcuts (read inaccuracies) or one had automated the process. CAMS had already determined that manually dealing with public issues was near impossible and had taken steps towards automating the entire process. Its background in the IT services business, of course, did help. Only three companies survived what became known as the 'electronic' crisis, because the only way to adhere to the new SEBI norms was to go electronic in the processing. They were Link Intime, Karvy and CAMS. The remaining 147 or so companies that had been doing this task manually either shut down voluntarily or were forced to shut down due to loss of business.

Mutual funds were launched around that time. The early entrants into a nascent Indian market launched the product, which promptly got mistaken for yet another public issue. Consequently, the response was muted, and the market had to lick its wounds and re-examine strategy for entry. Integrity apart, CAMS was also able to build a reputation for timely and accurate delivery within the seventy-day deadline. The foreign mutual funds which were entering the Indian market for the first time wanted a reliable partner, and CAMS fit the bill perfectly.

CAMS set itself two goals:

How do we treat any investor anywhere in the world on par?

How do we ensure that all customers anywhere in India have access to identical information?

In addition, mutual funds wanted the information in one hour, as per prevailing standards abroad, but banks were taking five days. CAMS then opened offices in seven cities, and these cities were giving nearly 95 per cent of the share subscriptions. Customers outside these seven cities had a lag time of three days.

In 1999, CAMS decided to exit the share registry business and focus only on mutual funds. It was a tough decision to take, with the share repository business just about peaking. That decision enabled CAMS to dominate the mutual funds business, and today, over 80 per cent of the mutual funds business passes through CAMS.

We ask Shankar—who is on the verge of exiting most of his shareholding in CAMS as he settles down to become a model grandfather—what advice he would give to new start-ups. Here's what he said:

i.   It takes time to become a company and it would be imprudent to have expectations like 'becoming a unicorn in three years'. Focus on ensuring that you have a saleable product first.

ii. Be cognisant of value systems. Have a lofty goal and ensure that you strive to achieve it with practice while you preach it. Big things don't matter, but small simple ones do. Set an example to your colleagues.

iii. It is good to operate with spare thinking capacity in the organization. It calls for some level of training and inputs to teach your colleagues that you value their inputs. But you also need to be able to afford this spare thinking capacity. A careful selection of mentors might suffice, especially during early days.

Three characteristics that we observed about this entrepreneur: he is highly focused on his business, sets very high standards, and is very modest and humble.

8.   Software as a Service (SaaS): Girish Mathrubootham

What makes Girish tick is a question that is foremost in the minds of several young entrepreneurs who look up to him. Having won a Start-up of the Year Award, with $150 million annual recurring revenue (ARR), Girish represents the promise that Chennai will emerge as the SaaS capital of India. This is with good reason, considering that companies such as Zoho have set a scorching pace and a unique business model. In fact, Zoho is an alma mater of Girish who earned his spurs there. Born and schooled (Campion School) in Trichy, Girish is the true small-town boy who has arrived in the global marketplace.

Naru has clear memories of his association with Girish, 'I first met Girish at one of the early jigs at the Startup Centre when he had just got started. I did not quite understand what Freshdesk was all about, and Girish did not try too hard to explain it to me either. He did not find it necessary to sell me the idea and with good reason. And I understand why now, as investors queue up to invest in Freshworks. Recent fund raise of $150 million on a valuation of $3.5 billion puts Girish firmly in the unicorn saddle. As usual, we run into each other at TCA, and coincidentally at the Madras Club. Yes, he too is an early morning walker along with his charming wife Shoba. The family has relocated to the US as Girish primes himself up for an IPO in 2021/22.'

After engineering placement was over in February 1996, Girish went to the Ayyappan temple and wrote a letter to God. 'Where do I go next?' was what he asked. As it turned out, he was the last person to get admission into the MBA class of 1998 at Madras University. But Girish has had a colourful career on his way to the global marketplace. He worked in HCL–Cisco and conducted a corporate training programme for Polaris. 'I was petrified,' he admits, 'but I knew that I had to go through with the training programme.' Even while he was in college, for a fee of Rs 18,000, he trained six of his friends in Java. After the Polaris training programme, Girish was convinced that he was destined to train and he rented a place and started a training school. Friends brought their friends for training and Expert Labs got off the ground.

Girish's father worked for a public sector bank and his childhood was a motherless one as his parents got divorced when he was just seven years old. His father remarried around three years later and his relationship with his stepmother was uneasy. A tough childhood only helped to make Girish a calm and caring human being.

Today, Girish is the CEO of what could be India's largest product company in the global marketplace. Freshworks (previously known as Freshdesk) provides a suite of products and one could argue that Girish was competing head to head with his previous employer Zoho. But his eyes were on a target—the global market leader Zendesk. Accel Partners was the first to give Freshdesk a term sheet and Girish sweated while he struggled to meet the payroll when Accel took a 2.5-month period before releasing the first cheque.

But his target remained unchanged amid all this turmoil. Zendesk termed Freshdesk as a 'rip off of Zendesk' and Freshdesk was described as a 'bunch of Indian cowboys'. But some of these critics had not even seen Freshdesk and this was exposed in a site called ripoffornot.org, created by none other than Girish himself. But the contents of the site went viral and this became one of the biggest advertisements for Freshdesk. While Zendesk addressed the top end of the enterprise market and worked its way downwards, Freshdesk addressed the bottom end of the market, and worked its way upwards. A head-on collision is yet to happen but a healthy respect for each other already exists between the two companies.

Girish values his experience at Zoho and believes that this experience is what that has made him what he is. In any case, it is true that Zoho has given birth to several start-ups in the B2B space—either directly or has inspired them. And Zoho and Freshworks have been at the forefront of bringing Chennai to the position of the SaaS capital of India. And while the early noughties gave birth to several B2C start-ups in India, it would appear that the time has come for B2B product companies, a segment in which Freshworks is a forerunner.

Girish is quite an unassuming personality. But he loves the good life as evidenced in his acquisition of four cars, three of which are Mercedes-Benz. But although Freshworks commands a valuation of $1.5 billion, Girish is possessed with the idea of making at least 1000 of his early employees into dollar millionaires. And to achieve this goal, he would have to guide his company into a $10 billion valuation and in addition plan an IPO on NASDAQ. And with that mission in mind, Girish will most likely relocate himself to the US for the next few years with bag and baggage and family—as a host of new challenges lie ahead of him.

Here are a few interesting things you need to know about him.

- Girish is an ardent fan of Rajnikanth and his office has several posters of Rajnikant. By his own admission, he found himself speechless on the one occasion that he saw Rajnikant face to face. Some of the much-publicized humility that Rajnikant displays has worn off on Girish. He is a modest man with no airs about him.
- He is single-mindedly focused on getting to the top of the heap in the business suite vertical.
- He is a family man, with two boys aged fifteen and thirteen years, and accompanies his wife every day (when he is in Chennai) for a walk.

He is an icon for the average Tamil IT professional. And hopefully, he is about to make India proud.

9. Orangescape: Workflow Management for Suresh Sambandam

Suresh is another entrepreneur whom Naru has known. Naru recalls, 'I first met Suresh Sambandam at a TiE event. Both *Crossing the Chasm* and *Blue Ocean Strategy* are recorded as books that influenced his thinking. I myself am an avid fan of both authors. So, there you are. Mutual interests were quickly established and we both gravitated towards a group that was keen to do something for start-ups in Chennai. We were founding members of the Startup Centre in Chennai. I was one of the Angels that Suresh accosted even as early as when Orangescape was focused on 'Platform as a Service' (PaaS), and I had no hesitation in investing in his company. We had a rendezvous in Silicon Valley when Suresh was trying to market his PaaS. He had totally integrated into the US culture when we met at a Starbucks in the Valley. At that time, news was just trickling in on the initial and positive response to Kissflow. Picking up from where we left off was smooth and easy when he returned to India to pursue Kissflow more diligently.'

Orangescape is also a Chennai-based company. It is also a SaaS company. And it also offers a product to the enterprise. And also sells primarily to the US market. Suresh is a native of Cuddalore in Tamil Nadu.

He is also quite well read. *Crossing the Chasm* by Geoffrey Moore, *The Fifth Discipline* by Peter Senge and *Blue Ocean Strategy* by Kim Chan are the three books you could read to gauge what shaped Suresh. Even if you have no interest in what shaped him, you cannot really go wrong by reading this fine selection. And it is a pleasure to talk to and listen to him as he weaves his entrepreneurial life story in and out of one or the other of the above books.

As is often common in the south, he is soft-spoken and modest with a fine sense of humour (although he raucously and loudly laughs at his own jokes sometimes). He started Orangescape in 2004, obsessed with the idea of developing a PaaS product. All entrepreneurs are driven by the belief that they have conceived a product or story whose time has come. Suresh was no exception. At the time, he was convinced that the time for PaaS had come. And Orangescape started off with a product called 'Dimension', a client server version of PaaS. They launched it and waited for orders to come. The Indian Angel Network saw the possibilities and along with a couple of independent angels from Chennai seeded Orangescape with one million dollars. Suresh agreed to relocate to the US where the main market was expected to be.

By Suresh's own admission, PaaS did not belong to any known category and Orangescape did not have any marketing strategy in place. A strong bet on a technology that did not mature fast enough. And with not enough thought given to the role of cloud that was not yet clearly visible then, Orangescape was already deep into implementation before they realized that PaaS could simply not happen in any reasonable time span.

In 2008, Google launched PaaS—GAE (Google App Engine), primarily aimed at programmers. Between 2009 and 2013, Orangescape persisted with PaaS. It was selling but not scaling. Wipro was an early customer. They were able to reduce development on a 'reverse auction product' from eighteen months (internal estimate) to six months using the Orangescape platform. Suresh even optimistically relocated to Bangalore from Chennai. But gradually the acceptance of PaaS declined. Very simply put, the cost of selling was too high.

Orangescape attempted to sell to the global market. A UK inquiry converted into a personal visit by Suresh. The purchase price was finally negotiated for £90,000. When Suresh went to meet Cliff Burroughs, the CMO at UniBic, Cliff mentioned a project called Pixelperfect where the user interface alone was stated as the justification for a price of £50,000. That meeting was a revelation for Suresh. It hit him between the eyes then that without a perfect user interface, he had no chance in the global marketplace. And the opportunity too was presented on a platter by Cliff, who added that he intended to use the PaaS platform for a series of mini workflows. And so, Kissflow was born. And the rest is history in the making.

Google reached out to jointly develop a workflow platform that could eventually go on to the app store. The original idea of PaaS in the app store got compromised to workflow in the app store. And Rahul Sood, the Orangescape champion within Google, left Google around the same time as the PaaS reality struck home. In theory it was back to the drawing board, except some progress had been made on Kissflow. Today, and several years later, Kissflow has crossed some milestones with a near double digit ARR that leaves Orangescape with a positive bottom line. And Suresh has also been at the forefront of sharing his theses on selling to the US market and encouraging B2B start-ups to offer a SaaS product. In no small way, Suresh and Girish have been contributing to the emergence of Chennai as the SaaS capital of India.

A positive bottom line has emboldened Orangescape to offer a suite of adjacent products that could be offered to existing customers.

This chapter walked the reader through brief narratives of nine start-ups, imagined as being from the wild. The common lessons from these stories are summarized as the concluding part of the chapter titled 'The Call of the Wild'. India has the third-largest start-up ecosystem in the world. There are over 6000 start-ups registered with the Startup India Foundation, a not-for-profit foundation set up by a group of entrepreneurs. There are many stories to tell, and more importantly, many more stories to be heard.

The next chapter comments on selected aspects of the changing landscape for entrepreneurship in India. Reading through the anthology of developments influencing the entrepreneurial landscape, the reader will realize that while the terrain is still uncertain, it is not one to be ignored.

3

Changing Landscape

The Evolution of Silicon Valley

We have a young friend, Amit Sridharan, who now lives in Silicon Valley. He worked at Tata after his graduation from IIM Lucknow, resigned to study at Stanford and started to work with Mahindra in the Valley. The subject of his essay[1] on the origins and evolution of Silicon Valley is highly relevant to this book. Sridharan writes:

> The Silicon Valley as we know it today was a rural economy. It was Fred Terman, the Stanford Provost, also known as the father of Silicon Valley who built the base for the hi-tech industry in the West. Fred Terman was 10 years old when he moved to Stanford with his parents. The stage was set as the young man received his Engineer Degree in electrical engineering from Stanford. He then headed east to MIT. In those days, Terman recalled, 'a serious young engineer had to go back east to put

---

[1] Amit Sridharan, 'Look Beyond the Valley', Magzter, https://www.magzter.com/article/Business/Indian-Management/Look-Beyond-The-Valey

spit and polish on his education.' He earned a Ph.D. in 1924 at MIT.

At the age of 24, doctorate in hand, he returned home to the Stanford campus to spend the summer. He planned to join the faculty at MIT in the fall as a new assistant professor. Instead, tragedy struck; he developed a serious case of miliary tuberculosis. Terman spent the next year in bed, with sandbags on his chest. There was no specific treatment for tuberculosis at the time and he accepted a part-time teaching position at Stanford.

As his health recovered and he grew to becoming a full-time professor and later the dean of the engineering school, Terman attracted strong government funding post the World War II era to Stanford. Terman was thus able to attract bright new faculty and students to the West. He was also very involved with students and encouraged them towards entrepreneurship. In addition, he continued to encourage his graduates to start their own companies. Faculty members soon joined in consulting, investing, and, in some instances, founding new companies. Terman believed in building an eco-system that fused Government funding, University research and Industry. In 1951, this led to the setting up of the Stanford Industrial park where many of the early semiconductor companies built their offices.

In 1939, William Hewlett and Dave Packard, students at Stanford, encouraged by Terman, founded Hewlett-Packard out of a garage in Palo Alto, which originally made oscilloscopes. Then, during World War II, HP made radar and artillery technology.

In the 1940s, William Shockley co-invented the transistor while at Bell Labs. The transistor is now known as the computer processor. In 1956, Shockley left Bell and founded his own company—Shockley Semiconductor Labs. It was the first company to make transistors out of silicon and not germanium. The company was founded in Mountain View, California—so Shockley could be closer to his sick mother. Terman convinced

Shockley that he should set up the company in the Bay Area and Shockley's company employed many recent grads of Stanford.

In 1957, eight Shockley employees grew tired of his demeanor and left the company. Shockley called the group the 'Traitorous Eight.' They partnered with Sherman Fairchild to create Fairchild Semiconductor. In the early 1960s, Fairchild helped make computer components for the Apollo program. This led to the birth of the semiconductor industry.

Later in the decade, many of the 'Traitorous Eight' left Fairchild and founded their own companies. Including Gordon Moore and Robert Noyce who in 1968 founded their own company in Santa Clara called Intel. Soon after, other ex-Fairchild employees and 'Traitorous Eight' members helped found AMD, Nvidia, and venture fund Kleiner Perkins.

In 1969, the Stanford Research Institute became one of the four nodes of ARPANET. A government research project that would go on to become the internet. In 1970, Xerox opened its PARC lab in Palo Alto. PARC invented early computing tech, including ethernet computing and the graphical user interface. In 1971, journalist Don Hoefler titled a 3-part report on the semiconductor industry 'SILICON VALLEY USA'. The name stuck.

Thus, the foundation of the Silicon Valley was based on three principles

i.   The rebels who moved into the barren west, both researchers and entrepreneurs who initially had meagre resources but a deep desire to be successful.
ii.   The early realization of the importance in building a mutually reinforcing relationship between university and the surrounding community (government and industry).
iii. A continuous wave of entrepreneurs who could evolve with technology in Hitech from radio technology to

semi-conductors to micro-chips and become the centre of the personal computer revolution.

Features of the Silicon Valley model—what makes it work?

Creation of an Eco-system—Importance of Universities in driving Innovation and Entrepreneurship:

Between 2006 and 2017, Stanford University and UC Berkeley together, had 2216 entrepreneurs, founding 1918 companies, raising $39.7 Bn in capital (Pitch book Universities Report, 2017). This was much higher than any other place in the world.

The entrepreneurial bug is so strong in these universities that the admissions process tends to model the intake based on the candidate most suited to follow the dream of entrepreneurship. The questions in the application process are geared towards understanding the deeper motivations of the individual towards their greater purpose. Stanford Business School defines its purpose as 'Change Lives, Change Organizations, Change the World'.

The professors, lecturers and researchers in the universities are encouraged to collaborate extensively with industry. Many of them join back after successful stints in the industry and end up being mentors and investors to start-ups that emerge out of the campuses. The teaching roles so fluid that professors can run and establish companies while meeting their academic requirements. Many times, lead students or researchers working with professors collaborate to start a company. Stanford has a strong IP license policy where the research coming out of the university can be taken private by paying a fee. Patenting licensing technology coming out of university labs to benefit the university as well as the inventors. The recombinant DNA technology coming out of Stanford led to the birth of biotech industry. Stanford University labs gave birth to the likes of

Google and VMware and Stanford still holds stakes in these listed organizations.

This collaboration between the university labs—professors, students—helps magnify the effort required for the innovation. Every year, Stanford has almost 22 per cent of its students completing the PhD program every year, UC Berkeley will have a similar number. From 1950 to 1970—the population of Silicon Valley tripled in two decades from 3,00,000 to 1 million people. One new person was moving into the Valley every fifteen minutes for twenty years straight. Now we're at the point where two-thirds of the people working in science and technology in the Valley today were born outside the U.S. More than half of the so-called unicorn companies that are privately held with a valuation of a $1 billion or more have someone born outside the U.S. as a founder or co-founder. You don't have Silicon Valley without its focus on diversity.

This focus on diversity also leads to increasing collaboration across different disciplines to create innovation in different fields. It is not uncommon for Stanford Business School students to 'go across the street' and take classes at the engineering or design or medical school. This cross-pollinates ideas and exchanges amongst students of different disciplines and there are many examples of start-ups emerging out of this collaboration. Many business school students look for technology partners from the PhD or Masters programs across different schools. Within this closed and safe network provided by Stanford, students often find their business co-founders Jorge Heraud came to business school with deep industry insights in agriculture and wanted to build a machine that can identify weeds and do automated spraying of weedicides. During the year, he spent time looking for a co-founder in computer vision who can help him build this technology. He found his partner in the PhD program and started Blue River Technologies. The company, which is now acquired by John Deere, is leading the technology development in precision spraying.

Courses within many of the programs are also structured to encourage this behaviour where cross-registration across schools is given preference. The faculty encourages students to form diverse groups often, to promote and spark innovation. There are entrepreneurial labs and courses as part of the curriculum that are designed to teach and incubate start-ups. For example, the business school has programs called 'start-up garage' where students are encouraged to join not with a fully formed idea but a broad theme which they would like to explore. The team then spends the entire quarter doing field work and nailing down the idea. There are specific labs designed to help students think about building and scaling technology start-ups in the engineering school. Steve Blank, who pioneered the concept of learn start-up methodology, offers a course every winter and spring on helping students build a lean start-up. Getting into the course is competitive and has a selection bar that teams must meet to be part of the course. The pre-selection, early exposure and resources provided in such courses, help the students to kick-start their entrepreneurial journey while they are in school.

There are also supporting grants provided by the school for ideas that are ground-breaking and have a larger impact on the world. These are substantial grants that allow students to incubate the company and attract high-quality multi-disciplinary talent to join the company. While in school, Himanshu and his team were looking to build an AI-based product around climate change. To fund the initial prototype, he received funding from Tom-Kat Foundation to hire interns from Stanford to work on this over the summer. This initial funding led to significant contributions in data science and helped him incorporate the company.

Interestingly, there is an entire eco-system that has developed that focuses on the same construct, not only inside the university but surrounding it as well. StartX is an accelerator that only sponsors students from Stanford with a backing of one of the professors or researchers. Micro venture capital firms like Pear VC, tend to focus extensively on funding companies which have been founded by students who have just come out of the Stanford campus. Lawyers and legal firms also visit campuses to make an informal introduction to the students so that they can find their pathways to the real world without any hiccups. The idea is to build on the eco-system that has already been established by the university and giving it wings to fly in the outside world.

Like with many things in life, it is not the presence of a single element but a combination of several elements that makes for success of this eco-system. Many of these elements are mutually reinforcing. For example, StartX or Pear VC will not exist if Stanford students did not focus on entrepreneurship or seek funding in the early stages of setting up their businesses, yet at the same time, their existence enables the students, who have just stepped out of these campuses, significant collaboration with the external world.

Frenetic Innovation: Passing the Baton

Steve Jobs in his commemoration speech at Stanford University in 2005, mentioned the importance of passing the baton in the culture of Silicon Valley. When he was removed from Apple, he felt that he had dropped the baton that had passed down from Dave Packard (HP) to Bob Noyce (Intel) to him.

This probably could be another reason why the Silicon Valley, time and again, has been at the centre of technical disruptions. As technology has continued to evolve, from semi-conductors to micro-chips to personal computers to smart phones to Cloud to AI, the Valley's innovations have continually been built on the foundation of a previous generation of entrepreneurs. For example, while we know Steve Jobs and Steve Wozniak started Apple, Wozniak being the senior talent in the semi-conductor industry moved into the top management of the company.

Even in recent times, as machine learning, multi-core architecture or robotics have taken root, people in the Valley have been progressing from one kind of technology to the other. These founders have thought boldly and innovatively about how to monetize different services and products. Many new business models around SaaS, like network effects and freemium (where one gives the basic service free and charges for higher-end usage) have emerged from the Valley.

The idea of innovation in the Valley is about disruption but there is greater value in repeating the success of building technology companies at a global scale. While everyone believes that Silicon Valley is great for start-ups, few realize that it's real value comes from scale-ups. Hence, most often, the business models or technology that emerges out of the Valley is usually fast-scaling technology.

This is where the eco-system of successful entrepreneurs and venture capitalists, has been able to give the right mentorship and advice on rapid scaling or 'blitzscaling' (a term coined by Reid Hoffman). The kind of growth involved in blitzscaling (tripling in headcount each year isn't uncommon) requires a radically different approach to management than that of a typical growth company (which would be happy to grow 15 per cent per year). Companies that blitzscale have to rapidly navigate a set of key transitions as their organizations grow, and have to simultaneously focus on customer success.

The interesting aspect is that the eco-system mentioned earlier broadly sets the filters on the kind of ideas that will get experimented in the Valley. For example, a brick and mortar product or distribution business with no technology or patent interface has very low probability of being funded in the Valley even if it makes an attractive financial model. Venture capitalists will not fund ideas that do not fit their model for scale-up. During the selection of students to Stanford, the university looks to the students to explain why they want to be in the Stanford eco-system rather than others, possibly filtering out the people who will better fit into the Valley. So, even within the diversity that the Valley tries to create, it still looks for people who have a focus for technology-led solutions. The ability of the Silicon Valley to focus on its strengths in just building fast-scaling technology business repeatedly is probably unique to its culture.

Tolerance for Risk and Failure

The initial journey of any idea also includes milestones. For any start-up, the test starts with building an MVP. The concept of Minimum Viable Product (developing a product with the least amount of resources in the shortest possible time to test and iterate in the market) is well-accepted as proof point for the idea. The early iterations around innovation, according to Reid Hoffman, is like 'throwing yourself off a cliff and assembling a plane on the way down'.[2] You probably won't get it right the first, second or third time around. But you keep going. The key is to learn from your failures. Try, fail, learn, and try again.

For any innovative idea to succeed, you need patience and you need people to back the founders. While the campus environments are safe for repetitive iterations, even in the real world, investors accept failure as learning and many entrepreneurs get funding even post a failed start-up. The entire venture capital industry is positioned towards accepting that not all ideas will succeed but the ones that do will compensate for

---

[2]   Drake Baer, 'How LinkedIn's Reid Hoffman Jumped Off A Cliff And Built An Airplane', FastCompany.com, 17 May 2013, https://www.fastcompany. com/3009831/how-linkedins-reid-hoffman-jumped-off-a-cliff-and-built-an-airplane

all failures. This idea of taking risks in making the investments, comes from the culture set by successful entrepreneurs who have reinvested their wealth into new ideas.

Entrepreneurs who have made substantial amount of money, set up their venture funds or become investors into funds that further their purpose. The start-ups benefit not only from the money but also the expertise of these founders and learn from their journey.

The ripple effect of people who are making money and at the same time investing it back into the same eco-system is what is fuelling the innovation and tolerance for risk in the Valley.

What can India learn from the Silicon Valley model?

Just like any human creation which is a combination of mutually reinforcing factors is difficult to replicate in another place, geographical portability of any model becomes difficult but not impossible. But business ideas are more portable than business models. For example, large-scale retail is a business model but in India it has not proven to be portable, but the idea that Indians want access to large scale retail is portable and many e-commerce companies have emerged to address this need.

The Silicon Valley phenomenon has two dimensions:

1. Frenetic innovation with new ideas
2. An ecosystem that defines the business model

While India will take many years to build an efficient eco-system like Silicon Valley, frenetic ideation is a portable business idea. Indians have the problem-solving ability which is the right genetic material for entrepreneurship.

India could look at creating a business model on two dimensions that follow a different approach from Silicon Valley:

1. Much like the way India has established itself in IT services, Indian innovativeness can be used as an outsourcing

device—Indian start-ups can generate the ideas at a low cost and transfer to markets like the US. Indians have the advantage of having a large pool of technical talent, which can innovate, but don't have the right eco-system to scale up to a large enough market to expand their hi-tech solutions locally. By finding an approach for cross-over to developed markets post-incubation, Indian innovativeness could in itself become a business to be extended to the rest of the world?. Can venturing become the next export?

2. Work to direct the Indian innovation on problems which India uniquely faces. India has a unique set of problems that we face in areas like health and education. Indian Venture Capitalist (VC) money could be channelized to scale up solutions addressing these problems. One can also learn some lessons from the evolution of Chinese VCs who started by replicating others but later followed their own model.

India's Accelerating Start-up Culture

By the 1960s, some data work was already being undertaken in a group like Tata under US-returned Lalit Kanodia, Yash Sahni and some others. On 1 April 1968, Tata Consultancy Services (TCS) was set up—with that name and style—as a division of Tata Sons. Among post-Independence start-ups, TCS has emerged as India's most valuable company and is a symbol of Indian entrepreneurship. Before words like pitching, venture capital and series 'A' were invented, a forty-four-year-old MIT-trained engineer called F.C. Kohli 'pitched' to the investment committee of Tata Sons—J.R.D. Tata, Nani Palkhivala, Freddie Mehta and P.M. Agarwala.

Several hugely successful start-ups with distinctly Indian models have grown up over the many decades—TCS, Infosys, Wipro, Bharati Airtel in the technology sector; Reliance, HDFC Bank and Titan in the traditional sector. These grown-ups can now offer lessons for wannabe start-ups.

According to World Bank India head, Junaid Kamal Ahmad, India has the potential to 'do a Silicon Valley within five years'. However, Silicon Valley has no cultural connection with India. Can it work?

We pondered over the question: Is India's culture of entrepreneurship accelerating?

Recent researchers point out, as indeed does the World Bank, that any entrepreneurial society requires an ecosystem that is embedded in the unique heritage and culture of that society. According to Professor Daniel Isenberg, founding executive director of Babson Entrepreneurship Ecosystem Project, several elements comprise the ecosystem. If the elements are individually improved, ecosystem effectiveness is reduced, according to Professor Isenberg. 'Together, however, these elements turbocharge venture creation and growth.'[3]

Academicians Eric Stam and Ben Spigel of the University of Edinburgh also note that 'the ecosystem is a set of *interdependent* actors and factors coordinated in such a way that they enable productive entrepreneurship within a particular territory'.[4]

Such a culture would mean a *wide* social acceptance of entrepreneurship as a laudable activity. In some cultures, children are not expected to become entrepreneurs. It may come as a surprise to parents of Chettiar, Marwari or Bhatia communities if their ward joined Tata or Infosys. The opposite happens when a middle-class Tamil or Bengali Brahmin wishes to start a business. Widespread acceptance means that society welcomes start-ups. The cultural element improves with networking and social ties, supportive government policies and social approval

---

[3]   Daniel Isenberg, 'The Big Idea: How to Start an Entrepreneurial Revolution', *Harvard Business Review*, June 2010, https://hbr.org/2010/06/the-big-idea-how-to-start-an-entrepreneurial-revolution

[4]   Erik Stam and Ben Spigel, 'Entrepreneurial Ecosystems' in Blackburn, R., De Clercq, D., Heinonen, J. & Wang, Z. (Eds), *Handbook for Entrepreneurship and Small Business* (London: Sage, 2017), https://dspace.library.uu.nl/bitstream/handle/1874/347982/16_13.pdf

of the activity. With the emergence of city angel networks TiE and YPO, nowadays, there is considerable energy in the swirling entrepreneurial undercurrents.

Changing a deeply ingrained culture is enormously difficult. Other societies have demonstrated that it is possible to alter social norms *in less than one generation*. In Ireland and Chile, as in Silicon Valley, Boston and Israel, entrepreneurs learnt that it is possible to fail, regroup and to try again. A good test for discerning whether start-ups are accepted in India is to ask whether it is all right to fail and try again—India is not quite there yet. Indian society has not yet reached the stage where dropping out of college to start one's own business could be encouraged, but we may not be too far away.

From the 1960s until the new century, the shift from vying for government service towards professional management sprung strong roots. People would flaunt a foreign academic credential on their CV—an MIT degree, Harvard diploma or an international posting, all hallmarks of distinction and accomplishment.

For the new millennium generation, slowly and at an accelerating pace, it is attractive to harbour a start-up ambition. It is stylish to announce, 'I am on my third start-up.' Start-up as a vocation is still suspicious to the parents when a young man seeks the hand of someone's daughter. An acid test of social acceptance will be when parents are delighted to have a son-in-law running a start-up; that may not be far off in time.

That there is an intergenerational transformation should not surprise anyone, but the oncoming tsunami of accelerating cultural change could well surprise us.

Dandi March for Entrepreneurship

Small streams become mighty rivers. Atomic particles gather speed in a particle accelerator. Even bacteria rapidly multiply in suitable conditions. When people come together for a common cause, movements develop.

Gandhi-ji set out from Sabarmati Ashram on 12 March 1930 to protest the colonial salt tax with just a few people, but the crowds swelled uncontrollably en route to Dandi.

India began grassroots innovation in 2000, when IIM Ahmedabad's Professor Anil Gupta established the National Innovation Foundation with support from the department of science and technology. In 2015, a committee chaired by Harvard's Professor Tarun Khanna submitted a report on national innovation, inter alia, recommending a charter for Atal Innovation Mission (AIM). Within a brief time, AIM has executed actions on the ground and, for brevity, only some are mentioned below.

i. Atal Tinkering Labs (ATLs) are up and running—3000 already exist and the target was to set up 10,000 by end of 2020. Each 1500 sq ft ATL is equipped with do-it-yourself kits on latest technologies (IoT, Robotics, 3D printing). An ATL-in-charge and a mentor—2500 mentors have volunteered through a Mentor Networking Platform—both trained by AIM and its partners, are available to each ATL. In a recent ATL marathon, 35,000 school students from all over the country participated. Thirty projects have been selected for further development and support. A video clip showing the kids at work warms the cockles of the heart of every Indian—our kids are smart and are beacons for the future.

ii. Atal Incubation Centres (AICs) will help creative ideas from ATLs and other sources to be rigorously validated and nurtured. Nineteen AICs are already operational at existing universities and institutions with much larger numbers on the anvil.

iii. Much else has been planned. Every district in the country is targeted to have at least one ATL, so that school kids get deeply involved, early in life, with tinkering and ideating. Early intervention is the AIM mantra.

iv. The structure of AIM is not the usual advisory board that one is accustomed to. It bears the name MHLC, standing for Mission High Level Committee. Its members are the top leadership of

NITI Aayog along with half a dozen secretary-level officials from the government. The MHLC has private sector managers and thought leaders also as its members (here I must disclose that I, Gopalakrishnan, am one of the members).

In short, the name, charter, functioning and composition of the Atal Innovation Mission have been designed to be workman-like, with the use of modern management techniques—Balanced Score Card, Annual Targets and Project Review. The chief, called the mission director, is R. Ramanan, a former CEO/MD of CMC Limited. He has been generously seconded by Tata Consultancy Services. His bustling, young team cuts an impressive sight.

A Sabarmati equivalent may well be underway through NITI Aayog's AIM. Could AIM replicate the swelling Dandi crowds as it develops momentum over the next twenty years? If it does, it would be a landmark in the entrepreneurial journey of the nation!

The goal of Atal Innovation Mission is to use common people's creativity to solve problems—to develop and deliver sustainable and replicable solutions. Indians have a unique knack of overcoming their day-to-day obstacles with short-term solutions or quick fixes, often referred to as *jugaad*. The difference between jugaad and innovation lies in a deep crevice called sustainability and replicability. Nothing is assured and this is far from having gathered momentum. However, the building blocks are getting into place; there is energy and commitment to move ahead, and hence reason to remain optimistic. In national public discussions on business innovation, Indians argue for a reorientation of social attitudes, modernization of school teaching and supportive government policies. These points are important to be raised and discussed but a course of action remains unclear after such discussions are over. AIM has adopted an approach that cuts across the apparent impediments and tries to use their strengths without getting bogged down in their weaknesses. Schools, universities, state governments and central government are not adversaries in this effort, but collaborative partners in this movement.

William Maloney, a World Bank chief economist, has recently co-authored *The Innovation Paradox* with Xavier Cirera, in which they have argued that developing countries must focus on a sound ecosystem and capability development. AIM has the potential to do for Indian innovation what Operation Flood did for milk production and Green Revolution did for agriculture; that must be its philosophy.

The motto of the mission is to Think Big, Start Small, Fail Fast and Move Quick.

Can Start-Ups Really Impact the Economy?

Truth be told, the real impact of start-ups begins with an IPO. That is why, if we consider e-commerce start-ups, the time horizon to impact could take a decade or more. Surely, technology can and will impact, for example, India's health-care and education access issues in the long run. Important folks in business and administration assert that current start-ups are India's hope to stimulate employment and spur national economic growth; their view appears persuasive, but we don't believe it is true.

Most likely, it is case of the emperor not wearing any clothes. Digital technologies are disruptive[5] and important; they could build a great future. However, it is unwise to expect nascent start-ups to shift the national needle for growth or job creation in the immediate future.

The valuations of start-ups we are seeing now reflect hubris, not business performance. In the next decade and more, economic growth and job creation will require renewed industrial investment, fresh lending by the NPA-strapped banks and a revival of the agricultural economy. These are grown-up dowdies, but they are the real movers and shakers of the economy. These sectors generate real cash, not

---

[5] Disruptive technology is an innovation that significantly alters the way that consumers, industries or businesses operate.

mythical valuations. Their cycle of production and consumption is based on real, stable money and experienced entrepreneurs. On the other hand, start-ups are based on ephemeral, impatient capital and inexperienced entrepreneurs, largely copycat local firms, slugging it out with foreign VC money. Scott Shane, professor of entrepreneurial studies and professor of economics at Case Western Reserve University, Ohio, wrote in 2014 that entrepreneurship does not cause income growth.[6]

Start-ups are abnormally growing corporate organisms. At least in India, most are unstable and unsustainable. Many are in the larval stage of the butterfly, when the insect continuously consumes mulberry leaves, adding bodily burdens and undergoing complex hormonal changes. Among Indian start-ups, you can count the number of butterflies that have emerged from the chrysalis, like Infosys and Bharti, but both are from three decades ago. During their infancy, these companies grew credibly with revenue, cost and profit surplus. These 'old start-up' companies spent hard-won investors' money frugally to prove their product, their business model and their commercials before undertaking rapid growth. Current start-ups measure performance through unintelligible metrics like Gross Merchandise Volume (GMV), app downloads and merchants on the platform, not through profits and Operating Cash Flow (OCF)!

There is far too much hoopla about Indian start-ups. Smart foreign VCs have arrived with their dollars, but smart people are known to sometimes behave mindlessly. There is an insane race to spend money to simulate the American dream of 'winner takes all' through an imported business model that the limited partners understand. Entrepreneurs argue that the losses are investments, yet they resent the income tax authorities treating the losses in that manner. The young and inexperienced entrepreneurs are called

---

[6]   Scott Shane, 'Entrepreneurship Doesn't Cause Per-Capita Income Growth', Entrepreneur.com, 23 September 2014, https://www.entrepreneur.com/article/237695.

upon to advise on the nation's economic policies and they adorn the juries to select daring leaders. However, they appeal for protection from muscular foreign boxers in the boxing ring, even though they themselves are owned by foreign capital.

Policymakers and followers of economic matters must listen to entrepreneurs as indeed to many segments of the population. But we must also listen to entrepreneurs who have a record of sustainably solving real consumer problems, servicing increasing customers, making investments in assets and generating jobs and cash. A minuscule number of today's start-ups will get there, but the time frame will be a decade or more. The corporate graveyard will be like a World War II cemetery with commemorative stones for the unheralded soldiers.

Young people are developing crazy apps because young people will be young! For example, apps that will pack your suitcase virtually, that will send a valet on a scooter to park your car wherever you may be, or a toothbrush to your mailbox to renew your dental kit regularly! And the media will go ballistic, the policymakers work up a froth, while the VCs chew their cigars purposefully awaiting an opportunity to sell to another VC in a ring-a-ring-o'-roses game.

Let start-ups be start-ups until they become grown-ups. Let young entrepreneurs be experimental and bold. Let VCs do their job. But for everyone's sake, the nation must prime the grown-ups to solve the imminent issues.

Hubris about Born-To-Be-Sold Start-Ups

We emphatically state the fact that start-ups are good for India. What we worry about is the hubris around start-ups as though they are the magical solutions to issues of economic growth and job creation. We worry that many start-ups are born to be sold.[7]

---

[7] Christian Livi and Hugues Jeannerat, 'Born to Be Sold? Start-Ups as Products and New Territorial Lifecycles of Industrialization', University of Neuchâtel, Switzerland, 2014.

Viewing start-ups as 'growing children' in our economic ecosystem, we wonder whether the children are growing all right, especially the e-commerce variety. There exist gullibility and infatuations, even at Silicon Valley, like Theranos and Juicero. After all, history is full of narratives about smart people collectively doing foolish things.

Is there too much hype about and around start-ups? Are many of these start-ups sustainable?

Here is why we are apprehensive. Trading and manufacturing economics are based on a centuries-old principle: for the investment of capital by an owner, there is revenue greater than cost, leaving some profit. To sustain the business (a new product or solution with a perceptible consumer benefit), competitive advantage must exist. Aware of the mortality of their business, owners aim for a quick recouping of their invested risk capital, depending on the nature of the business. It is this principle that is being torture-tested with the new players articulating, though not demonstrating, that the winner takes all. It is despairing to see a statement from the CEO of one of the most successful start-ups that its owners do not care about profit; they are only interested in market share! For how long? The company depends on muscling out others! Capital gets touted as a competitive advantage! The idea of predatory pricing is not new, and firms have experienced that during the last century, attracting laws like anti-trust and monopolies control.

The start-ups of the 1980s and 1990s, like Infosys and Bharti, aimed to make a profit within seven to eight years—and they did do so. The technology start-ups born 2001 onwards are estimated to have attracted investment of about Rs 3,00,000 crore ($45 billion). Cheered on by the media, and adorning award juries and national economic advisory councils, some entrepreneurs are celebrities, having earned an incredible amount of money in a very short time. With two arguable exceptions—Flipkart (with Walmart as parent) and MakeMyTrip (Chinese CTrip)—the question lingers: has any founder built a *sustainable* enterprise? Or have they just become rich like equity traders?

The acid test will be when their current financial investors want to exit. Will the companies be acceptable to the capital market for an IPO? Or to a long-term strategic investor? Current business models don't give confidence, and the mortality rate could well be huge.

It has been nineteen years since 2001, and we don't know if even one of the Indian start-ups has reached a positive cash flow status with a modicum of stability. If a bunch of traditional companies failed to turn in a sustainable positive cash flow, should it not ring alarm bells? Such companies become defaulters in due course, as the Indian economy is painfully experiencing. FMCG companies invest cash in advertising upfront, but the better companies maintain a tight vigil on its efficiency and returns. It may come across as an old-fashioned concern but with many of the successful technology start-ups, the end of the dark tunnel is not visible.

The Indian start-up movement cannot yet be classified as successful. When achieved, success can stimulate the economy through new consumer experiences and job creation. It will inevitably bring with it surprises and downsides. One such downside is hubris. Nobody wishes to miss this start-up party because the excitement arising out of technological changes and opportunities confirm that it's going to be a lively party. However, there needs to be more introspection regarding the aftermath of this party.

National economic benefit is not only about creating wealthy entrepreneurs, but also about creating long-living companies.

Start-Ups Need to Benefit the Have-Nots

Businesses have been regenerative for centuries. Many of today's established corporations began as start-ups. Modern start-ups are merely an alternative way to establish businesses as opposed to the traditional ways. They do so by increasing the degrees of freedom and agility in the initial stages and giving a freer rein to the founder's creativity. Adventurous enterprises have been enabled by a rather recent model of wealth as with venture capital and private equity models. Since the 1980s, the distribution of wealth developed differently from the 1950s, '60s and '70s.

Among the English-speaking nations, income inequality reduced after the Second World War until 1980 and then started rising again. In 1913, for example, in the US, UK and Canada, the share of the income going to the top 1 per cent was about 18–20 per cent. This share reduced to single digit by the 1980s; however, during the last forty years, the share of the top 1 per cent has risen sharply.[8] There was a gradual rise in the Gini coefficient in the US and UK between 1980 and 2013. According to a Brookings paper, authored by three Federal Reserve economists in 2016, the share of wealth owned by the top 1 per cent in America reached 33 per cent in 2012, though other economists estimated it even higher at 42 per cent. Whichever data you accept, the richest 1 per cent have gained disproportionately.

Since the 1980s, in pursuit of returns on wealth, the rich have sought risky ways to deploy their rising wealth. They sought new domains and geographies that would give them a better yield on their money. The rapid development of American venture capital and private equity owes a lot to the quest for a good return on this increasing wealth. The newly emerging technology space has provided the domain diversification sought by the wealthy. The dramatic economic changes in China and India have made those economies a natural magnet for a part of American wealth, providing geographic diversification to investors.

That which is a small part of rich American wealth is a big part of Indian foreign investment cash flows. The amount of foreign money entering India as Foreign Institutional Investor (FII) has grown fast in recent years, albeit on a small base. India receives about $5–6 billion of FII each month nowadays, a large part of which goes into public equity markets, but some amount into venture capital

---

[8] Max Roser and Esteban Ortiz-Ospina, 'Income Inequality', Ourworldindata. org, October 2016, https://ourworldindata.org/income-inequality

as well! Venture capital and private equity are driving start-ups and valuations of start-ups in India.

Earlier in this chapter, we had posited that the impact of start-ups, especially the digital ones, on India's growth and employment may not be significant over the next decade. We are sensitive to the view that arguments and facts must be stated in a way that is acceptable if one intends them to be meaningful. In short, the content of the message matters as much as its delivery. It is important for innovators to say the right thing in the right way. A great idea that is inadequately expressed faces rejection—think of the arguments married couples have, which are rarely about the content, but are about the manner.

Much of the benefits of the start-up ecosystem accrues to the 'haves', the privileged, the upwardly mobile youth. But it is the job prospects of the hundreds of thousands of the have-nots that dominates the national concern. Digital start-ups may not help in creating jobs for the underprivileged. Technology infrastructure solves many problems, but it cannot build roads, bridges or provide clean water. We need to be cognizant of the fact that job creation for the underprivileged is essential for human progress despite the fact that it requires big financial investments. China was able to progress as a country by recognizing that BAT (Baidu, Alibaba and Tencent) cannot do such things.

Start-Ups and Their Genes

Every species has a natural growth rate, determined by its genetics, metabolism and environment. Nature discourages artificial growth of any species beyond its necessities. Fruit flies don't try to become as big as cows, and cows don't try to become big like elephants.[9]

---

[9] R. Gopalakrishnan, 'Start-ups Grow in Line with Their Genes', *Business Standard*, 9 November 2017, https://www.business-standard.com/article/opinion/start-ups-grow-in-line-with-their-genes-117110901606_1.html

Max Kleiber, a Swiss-born academic at Davis, California, demonstrated in the 1930s that every species has, on an average, a stable number of heartbeats.[10] For example, the cow species is one thousand times heavier than the woodchuck species. Cows have a lifespan which is the 'square root of the square root of 1000', which is 5.5 times longer than the lifespan of the woodchuck species. The fruit fly lives only fifteen days compared to the heavy tortoise—it simply consumes its quota of heartbeats faster.

Could this logic apply to species of companies, which do behave, after all, like living beings? Like living beings, no two kinds of companies are the same. Steel companies are different from fast-moving consumer goods or media companies. Should entrepreneurial thinking recognize the biological nature of companies rather than treat companies as inanimate entities?

The Silicon Valley model of start-up technology companies requires extraordinary growth. This species is young, and its needs are not universally applicable. Their biology is not fully understood in respect of their metabolism, their heartbeats and their lifespan. Business management leaders understand the biology of traditional companies. Therefore, the appropriateness of the Silicon Valley model for Indian entrepreneurship is much debated.

According to trade estimates, foreign funding for Indian technology start-ups fluctuates wildly, from $8 billion in 2015, down to $4 billion in 2016, and up again to $10 billion in 2017. Three important points worth noting: first, this number is minuscule compared to what flowed into Chinese start-ups; second, the flow is influenced as much by international markets as by the excitement of the Indian start-ups per se; third, VCs are concentrating their Indian investments into fewer companies—Flipkart alone accounted for

---

[10] Reuben Westmaas, 'Almost Every Mammal Gets about 1 Billion Heartbeats', Discovery.com, 1 August 2019, https://www.discovery.com/nature/almost-every-mammal-gets-about-1-billion-heartbeats

40 per cent of the $10 billion inflow in 2017. At the stroke of a valuer's pen, Flipkart's value was diminished by a few billion dollars.

The Silicon Valley model certainly seems to work in the west and east coasts of USA, as also in China. A report demonstrates how China has surged ahead as a genuine technology innovator, besting American entrepreneurs at their own game.[11]

Common sense suggests that former founders would make better investors as VCs. CB Insights[12] crunched the data and found, to our great surprise, that non-founder VCs dominate the top ranks among VCs; further, that there is no relationship between the rank of top VCs and their experience as a founder. This is yet another evidence to doubt the depth of our collective understanding of the biology of start-up companies.

There are alternative and hugely successful models. The case of DMart, which started in 2002, is a good example of building an $8 billion enterprise in what might be considered a staid 1970s-style service industry of retailing. Radhakishan Damani (founder) does not attend corporate awards juries or advisory councils of the finance minister. DMart's CEO is also reported to have said that lofty ideas don't work in retail and that wins come from small incremental improvements pursued relentlessly.[13]

---

[11] Innovation Summit Asia 2018: Building the Intelligent Company, *The Economist*, 23 September 2018, https://events.economist.com/events-conferences/asia/innovation-summit-2018

[12] Dan Mindus,' Do Ex-Startup Founders Make the Best Venture Capitalists?', CBInsights.com, 23 October 2017, https://www.cbinsights.com/research/founders-best-venture-capitalist-investors/

[13] Samar Srivastava, 'DMart: The Juggernaut Continues to Roll for India's Value Shop', *Forbes India*, 24 October 2017, https://www.forbesindia.com/article/boardroom/dmart-the-juggernaut-continues-to-roll-for-indias-value-shop/48457/1

[R.] Gopalakrishnan, 'Start-ups Should Grow as per Their Nature', TheMindWorks.me, 10 November 2017, http://themindworks.me/2017/11/10/start-ups-grow-per-nature/

In that light, the statistics of Patanjali Ayurveda as stated in the media are impressive and media reports suggest the creation of another highly valuable company. Very little of published financial figures are available and what is printed appears suspect since the media always quotes round numbers for revenue and margin. The sceptics feel that there may be considerable bluster in the business profile that is being written about. Notwithstanding these views, the marketing chutzpah of bringing ayurvedic and natural products into central consciousness of consumers must accrue to this unusual company with unusual credentials.

As a writer observed, 'As with so much in India, the development of India's digital economy will be hard to predict, and resistant to convenient models plucked from elsewhere.'[14] Different pulse rates for different species of start-ups.

What Happens to the 'Wow' Innovations?

The two ends of the innovation journey—the early stage, which emphasizes creativity and cleverness, and the late stage, which emphasizes scaling and execution—are rich with literature, unlike the journey from one end to the other, which is scantier.

Consider the late stage first. Professor Ricardo Hausmann, a former minister in Venezuela and now director, Centre for International Development, Harvard University, argues that large organizations are better at research and development (R&D). Fruitful innovations emerge from large-scale R&D, and Hausmann quotes examples from Jon Gertner's 2012 book, *The Idea Factory*. His view is contrary to the popular view that small means more innovative and agile. Hausmann points out that trying to replicate a successful innovation ecosystem from one place to another is 'like

---

[14] Simon Mundy, 'Investors Back for Second Bite at Indian Tech', *Financial Times*, 24 October 2017, https://www.ft.com/content/4a74c6e0-b4bf-11e7-aa26-bb002965bce8

trying to build a bridge without the scaffolding. Complex ecosystems of innovation develop in each place because of idiosyncratic path development, distinctive in its own way'.[15]

The absence of an idiosyncratic innovation ecosystem is the reason why many nations, including India, are struggling with accelerating innovation. We rely on start-ups sans the ecosystem. Perhaps the ecosystem will develop in due course, but the hoopla about young people's ideas and start-ups would suggest that victory is in hand.

Consider the early and creative stage. In his comments on disruptive technologies at Fireside Chat hosted by Marico Innovation Foundation, Noshir Kaka of McKinsey states that they believe disruptive technologies will account for 20–30 per cent of India's incremental growth in the next ten years.[16] That is a big statement. Kaka may be right, but for his forecast to come true, the effectiveness of our Indian start-up ecosystem must be strongly visible already. We do not see that, not yet.

The Indian ecosystem faces tough issues in scaling up clever ideas and enticing solutions. Or else, by now, the clever ideas of a decade ago (reflect on the *Inventive Indians: 23 Great Stories of Change* by Ritu and Umesh Anand, published in 2009) would be viable, visible and impactful businesses.

Marico Innovation Foundation showcases winning ideas on MIF Talkies.[17] Rahul Rastogi's 'Sanket' has been presented as the world's only leadless, pocket-sized ECG monitor that can generate an ECG report in fifteen seconds. The creative idea is extremely well articulated

---

[15] Ricardo Hausmann, 'Large Organizations Are Better at R&D', LiveMint, 1 Dec 2017, https://www.livemint.com/Opinion/SMaNN5dpvXY5HVSMQCiR2J/Large-organizations-are-better-at-RD.htmlLarge organizations are better at R&D

[16] Marico Innovation Foundation, 'Disruptive Innovation - Fireside Chat Noshir Kaka', YouTube video, 21:25, 10 May 2016, https://www.youtube.com/watch?v=5HCqjhHa00Q

[17] Marico Innovation Foundation, 'MIF Talkies', 6 September 2017, https://www.youtube.com/playlist?list=PLQTw5BBZZRfie4L9rbOcqCUeyrvpCmpkV

and interesting. Dr Vishal Rao has designed a voice prosthesis device to enhance the lives of very poor people who lose their voice box due to ailments. His device will cost a fraction of the current models available. Narayen Peespathy of Bakeys has designed and developed edible cutlery, made of jowar and wheat. It resembles a wooden spoon, but it is not a wooden spoon. After eating your idli with hot sambhar, you can eat up the nutritious spoon, saving the environment the task of dealing with plastic cutlery. Far away in America, Chelsea Briganti's Loliware has designed Lolistraw—when you are done with your drink, you may eat the straw; don't throw it away!

All of these sound like truly innovative ideas and one cannot help feeling a thrill about the fact that India is blessed with youngsters with brilliant ideas. Akash Manoj is a fifteen-year-old boy, still in school in Tamil Nadu. He lost his grandfather to an undetected, silent heart attack. Resorting to the Internet, he designed a device to detect a protein called FABP3, which occurs in minuscule levels, but rises dramatically when heart conditions weaken. Fifteen-year-old Akash explains his idea so well that you cannot help feeling proud of his talent and feeling hopeful for India's future.

However, India does not have the ecosystem to take the brilliant ideas of these youngsters through all the stages from infancy and maturity. This may be because Indians are risk-averse. We suspect it is because India has no idiosyncratic innovation ecosystem, distinctively its own.

Our VCs will not rush to fund these ideas. They will individually applaud the ideas but will not be able to get the support of their American investment committees, which are looking to fund more American ideas like e-commerce, payment gateways and cab applications.

Entrepreneurs Plan and Plan, but Also Execute and Execute

It is silly to think that past entrepreneurs did not have a solid business plan or that a daring business idea alone matters, that there is no need to have a detailed plan.

The magnificent stories of the big four of Silicon Valley—Amazon, Apple, Facebook and Google—have provoked silly comments: for example, that the genius of great entrepreneurs is replicable through emulating their whims. The purchase of WhatsApp by Facebook for $19 billion in 2014 is quoted to suggest that founders should be allowed to act impulsively without the burden of consulting the directors; another example that raising funding through increasing valuations is key because the winner takes all. Here, we cover only the business planning aspect.

A couple of years ago it was the hundredth anniversary of the end of the First World War. It was a relevant date for the greatest entrepreneurial Indian venture, Tata Steel at Jamshedpur. We chanced upon a delightful old reprint of *A Steel Man in India* by John Keenan, published in 1945. John Keenan, an Irish–American from Gary, Indiana, worked in Jamshedpur from 1913 to 1938.

India was seen as elephants, tigers, maharajas. Where did steel fit in? The open-hearth process (of converting iron into liquid steel) was twenty years old, and steel was the hottest, hi-tech subject. India could weave textiles, but steel? Keenan accepted the challenge, and stayed for twenty-five years instead of his original plan of three years. Keenan lived at a time when he discussed matters with Dorabji Tata, the son of the founder, Jamsetji.

Dorabji's grandfather, Nusserwanji, had earned $1.5 million in 1867–68 through supply activities for Sir Robert Napier's campaign against the emperor of Abyssinia. This profit provided the venture funding to consider new and big ventures. Make no mistake, the venture was meticulously planned over ten years.

By learning from the iron-making experiences of Josiah Heath at Porto Novo, Madras (1830), Barakar Iron Works (1875) and Bengal Iron Works (1905), Jamsetji and Dorabji figured that the real competitive advantage and strategy lay in (a) getting advanced technology, (b) securing coal and iron ore as raw materials and (c) perseverance over the long haul. Planning these took them many years from idea to first production. Their three big secrets—planning, planning and planning.

To get access to contemporary technologies and technologists, Jamsetji set out to attend the 'World's Columbian Exposition' world fair held at Chicago in 1893. By the sheer passion in his eyes and sensitivity towards accommodating the needs of the 'foreigners', he attracted the likes of Charles Perin and John Keenan, among many others, to live and work in India.

Most importantly, Tatas trained Indians in steel-making, building a local organizational capability, which is even today the hallmark of Tata Steel! It was geologist P.N. Bose who found Sakchi at the fortuitous confluence of iron ore, coal and water. Perin employed the engineer's philosophy: build slowly and solidly; conserve your resources.

The project required mining permissions—ease of doing business was a big issue! While overcoming the restrictive laws, Jamsetji coped with the rebuffs of the then Viceroy of India, Lord Curzon, and had to approach the Secretary for India, based in London. Lord Hamilton was appalled at the manifold bureaucratic restrictions, so he actually instructed Lord Curzon to take the required action.

The First World War meant that the English and the French desperately needed steel. Tata expanded capacity, but not whimsically and certainly not without energetic planning. Between 1917 and 1920, Charles Perin dispatched to India about 7,00,000 tracings and three million blueprints. Soon after the war ended on 11 November 1918, Viceroy Lord Chelmsford said with undisguised admiration, 'I can hardly imagine what we would have done if Tata had not given us steel for Mesopotamia, Egypt, Palestine and East Africa.'[18] It would have been churlish of the British not to recognize Indian soldiers and Indian steel supplied for the First World War.

---

[18] John Keenan, *A Steel Man in India*, London: Victor Gollancz, 1945. Reprint, Hachette India, 2018.

Sound entrepreneurs who are building a business for the long term do plan in detail, which, as the Tata Steel example demonstrates, they revise and update frequently. Their techniques may appear primitive compared to later and more sophisticated planning techniques, but it would be naive to think that successful entrepreneurs do not plan and act impetuously.

This is an important lesson for modern entrepreneurs. In the frenzy of valuations and technology change, business planning should not become the casualty.

Public Procurement Can Support Innovation

In 2018, the Royal Air Force celebrated completion of a century in grand style all over the UK. However, nobody celebrated the fact that it was the RAF that gave a fillip to ballpoint pens.

Sixty-five ballpoint pens sell every second all over the world, year after year! The Hungarian inventor of the ballpoint pen, Laszlo Jozsef Biro, was included in the National Inventors Hall of Fame about eleven years ago. We were curious about what caused the innovation to take off.

While Biro had developed a working model of his ballpoint pen, he struggled to perfect his innovation. However, his work attracted the major powers of the Second World War. A British clerk suggested that airplane navigators who often had to make marks on maps while flying high above the ground, would benefit by the use of Biro's device. The British RAF placed a bulk order for 30,000 of Biro's ballpoint pens. This 'massive order' triggered lots of interest among inventors about the war effort. That was the beginning of the take-off of ball pens![19]

It is true that many Indians make startling innovations, but these innovators also need the equivalent of the RAF order.

---

[19] György Moldova, *Ballpoint*, New Europe Books, 2012.
R. Gopalakrishnan, *A Biography of Innovations*, Portfolio, 2017.

Pad Man, the movie, eulogizes the low-cost female hygiene product invented by Arunachalam Muruganantham. Forus Health has invented an eye screening device called 3netra—simple to use and far more affordable. Entrepreneur Rahul Rastogi has made a matchbox-sized ECG device called 'Sanket' as mentioned earlier. For how much? Rs 5. The list is almost as endless as it is inspiring.

These ventures do not take off because they struggle to get their first order. Government buying can give a fillip to such nascent innovations, but that too must be within a discipline of policies and processes. For example, government buying did not help Simputer.

The Simputer was released in 2002 as a self-contained, open hardware, Linux-based handheld computer. It had an attractive price of Rs 12,500 only. In 2004, Karnataka government used the Simputer to automate land records, Chattisgarh government used it for e-education and the police used it to track traffic offenders and issue traffic tickets. The key person behind Simputer, Swami Manohar, admitted that the innovation did not take off because of multiple factors—it was ahead of its time and it was not a failure because it showed Indians that hardware can be manufactured in India.[20]

Government buying, of course, can be made to work and be helpful. How? The regulations governing public procurement tend to be complex to keep government agencies honest, transparent and cost-minded. Therefore, if public procurement is to give the needed boost to innovations, the government must think through and articulate a clear policy. About ten years ago, the Swedish government commissioned its agency for innovation and its department for public procurement—Vinnova and Nou—to put their heads together and articulate a policy.

---

[20] N. Dayasindhu, 'What Lessons Does the Simputer Hold for Make in India?', FoundingFuel.com, 13 January 2017, http://www.foundingfuel.com/article/what-lessons-does-the-simputer-hold-for-make-in-india/

For India, as a starting point, reference may be made to the publication by EU Commission's directorate-general for industry and entrepreneurship publication for best practices in 'promoting innovation through public procurement'. Particularly in the public health arena of low-cost medical interventions and early diagnostics, this would have a potentially good pay-off to society.

Start-up Governance

Statistics in India are good but not robust; people's judgements are strongly influenced by their observations and intuitions, what they regard as truthiness. Hence, some believe that start-up governance is as poor as big companies, while others think that start-up governance can wait. Many people believe that most entrepreneurs are hucksters.

Truthiness and intuitive judgements need to be made through curated and careful observations. Hence, a director or funder of a start-up should have the experience and wisdom to judge entrepreneurial vision as well as execution capability.

Only one in tens of thousands of entrepreneurs may truly be a genius; the rest are ordinary blokes with dreams of finding this genius in them, and of them, only some are likely to be fraudulent. Entrepreneurs display behavioural characteristics in abundance— we call them 'prodromal signals', a bit like dark clouds and gusty winds which predicate an approaching storm. If behavioural prodromal signals abound, fund providers and directors need to be alert and be able to interpret them. These are well illustrated through the case of these companies: Theranos, and more briefly, Juceiro.

Theranos founder, Elizabeth Holmes,[21] is said to be a celebrated case of hubris, lying and opacity. She is known to have grown up

---

[21] John Carreyrou, *Bad Blood: Secrets and Lies in a Silicon Valley Startup*, Knopf, 2018.

in a wealthy family; constantly hearing stories about greatness, she became obsessive. Early in life, she figured that she wanted to make a lot of money. She displayed excessive competitiveness which manifested in tantrums with peers. She had a phobia of needles used to draw blood, so she diligently developed her distinctive idea that multiple tests could be done with just one pin prick of blood. Elizabeth dropped out of Stanford, an act that is associated with entrepreneurial brilliance by some. She even wore turtlenecks, emulating Steve Jobs.

Being driven, she leveraged her family connections to raise initial funds. Later with VCs, she resented probing questions about her technology—she is known to have gotten up and left in a huff when searching questions were posed by MedVenture experts. As Theranos grew, she is reported to have become unnaturally secretive—it is said even casual visitors to the company had to sign non-disclosure agreements. Jeff Hunter, a technical specialist, on the Walgreens delegation, was literally accompanied to the toilet to prevent his eyes straying around!

A few employees met the board chairman to express concerns about the ethics and bluster that was prevalent in the company. He had already heard some rumblings, so he quickly met the co-directors who all reached a consensus that Elizabeth should step down from being CEO because she was too inexperienced. They even communicated the board's decision to Holmes. Quite remarkably, she talked them into changing their minds. The directors failed to live up to the old adage: When you strike at a king, you must kill him.

Theranos achieved a valuation of $11 billion before it fell on its own sword. Elizabeth Holmes controlled a board of marquee names like Henry Kissinger, Sam Nunn and William Perry. As events panned out, she was indicted for blatant lying even while her company attracted increasing valuations from frenzied investors. She was a charmer of an exceptional quality.

Juicero, a Silicon Valley start-up, was founded by Doug Evans, who compared himself to Steve Jobs. The company was launched in

June 2016 and closed in September 2017 after a flattering profile in the *New York Times* and funding from the likes of Kleiner Perkins and Google Ventures. It remains a symbol of the Valley start-up culture that raises huge sums of money for solving non-problems!

We have noticed that many entrepreneurs come across as minor exemplars of these kinds of behaviour. We have noticed these five traits—inability to simplify, unwarranted confidence, slick-talking, name dropping and talking down.

The narratives of super ego and toxic behaviour among CEOs of large companies are disturbing and increasingly prominent. They seem to have a pattern. After the ascent, the CEO becomes powerful; power damages the brain, and the CEO's behaviour changes visibly. What can be seen is loss of empathy, arrogance, poor treatment of people and an inability to listen. Reference to these have been made in *Crash: Lessons from the Entry and Exit of CEOs*.[22] The derailers become the sword on which several CEOs fall. The CEO's downfall becomes 'breaking news' for the media, for example, Thomas Middelhof in Germany, Martin Sorrell in Britain, Carlos Ghosn in Japan and many in India.

It should not be assumed that power-induced brain damage applies only to CEOs of large companies. Founders and funders of start-ups are equally prone to this fatal affliction. Start-ups argue that they don't have the resources to monitor their adherence to numerous regulations and observing the codes of conduct. Obnoxious leadership behaviour and absence of work culture need to be extinguished with the same rigour as in large companies.

Just a couple of years ago, we witnessed the behavioural volatility of the key founder of Housing.com. He became abusive towards the funders of his venture; he is said to have behaved like a pampered and spoilt kid; the board had to dismiss him into anonymity. Paytm is portrayed as a successful start-up because the company has ratcheted

---

[22] R. Gopalakrishnan, *Crash: Lessons from the Entry and Exit of CEOs*, Penguin Random House India, 2018.

up well over 100 million customers in a short time. Many could argue that, with losses of several thousand crores each year, it could hardly *yet* qualify as a successful company. From a purely behavioural point of view, the rousing but foul, celebratory speech of the founder to the 4500 employees at a company party in 2017, after demonetization, is interesting to watch.[23] Judging by this evidence—admittedly a bit unfair—the soundness of the company leadership may well be an accident waiting to happen.

Start-ups are thought to provide the cool, better-behaved digital corporation of the future compared to the greedy, larger-than-life robber baron company of yesteryear. A new company today is expected to have a culture of being open, creative, inclusive, employee-friendly and geared towards solving the major consumer problems. The evidence for this perception is variable.

The older Silicon Valley ventures like Google and Facebook did attract great adulation during their run up to maturity; quite unexpectedly, they now attract social criticism and opprobrium. Jessica Powell's satirical novel (published on the digital platform Medium.com), *The Big Disruption: A Totally Fictional but Essentially True Silicon Valley Story*,[24] says a lot. The behaviour of founders of companies like Juicero, Zenefits and Theranos has managed to shake up non-expert observers who have been bewildered about how reputed VCs and family offices bought into ill-conceived or even fraudulent ideas, resulting in billions of dollars evaporating, right under their nose. Reid Hoffman, LinkedIn co-founder, has said that rapidly scaling companies need 'responsible blitzscaling' in his book *Blitzscaling: The Lightning-Fast Path to Building Massively Valuable Companies*,[25] co-authored with Chris Yeh.

---

[23] https://www.youtube.com/watch?v=0NvxdNodWDg
[24] Jessica Powell, *The Big Disruption*, Medium.com, 2019, https://disruption.medium.com/
[25] Reid Hoffman and Chris Yeh, *Blitzscaling*, HarperCollins, 2018.

In India, some commentators think that start-ups hold the key to the national issue of unemployment. The background and skills of those who need jobs contrasts with the atmosphere of start-ups like the e-commerce ones. The most admired e-commerce start-ups have modelled themselves on 'spend now, profits will follow' model. The jury is out about the likelihood of success, but that is essentially what entrepreneurship is. World Wide Web founder, Tim Berners-Lee, had warned, 'Humanity connected by technology is functioning in a dystopian way . . . online abuse, prejudice, bias . . .'[26]

Entrepreneurs have no choice but to shake a leg on the entrepreneurial dance floor, hoping that the music and their dance steps will sync at some point. Bill Gross, start-up entrepreneur and venture capitalist, analysed all the investments of his funds to determine the hierarchy of success factors. He found that timing is the most important success factor, not the idea, the team or the founder.[27] While start-up founders are tapping their feet on the dance floor, waiting for the right music, they should remember that good leadership behaviour and company culture in start-ups are just as important as in grown-up companies. Indian founders are a younger and more immature bunch compared to those in the US. With a fulsome media fawning on start-up leaders, Indian founders are exposed to a dangerous combination of derailers.

Start-ups Can Dance with Grown-ups

There is much happening in the Indian entrepreneurial space. We have wondered whether we would benefit by a more systematic

---

[26] Ian Sample, 'Tim Berners-Lee Launches Campaign to Save the Web from Abuse', *Guardian*, 5 November 2018, https://www.theguardian.com/technology/2018/nov/05/tim-berners-lee-launches-campaign-to-save-the-web-from-abuse

[27] TED, 'The Single Biggest Reason Why Start-ups Succeed: Bill Gross', Youtube.com, 6:40, 1 June 2015, https://youtu.be/bNpx7gpSqbY

development in an Indian innovation ecosystem, consistent with our cultural background. The transplanted Silicon Valley model can do only so much here. Every society has its own peculiarities, belief systems and ways of working.

There are several elements that define a national ecosystem. Prof. Mohanbir Sawhney of Kellogg School of Management, USA, is an experienced international academic. In a fascinating talk that I, Gopalakrishnan, attended, he counts at least ten elements in his broad definition of an 'innovation ecosystem': partners, institutions, alumni, professional societies, universities, government agencies, entrepreneurs, innovation marketplaces, industry cohorts and venture capitalists.

Another important aspect is the collaboration between start-ups and established companies. The case for this is self-evident—combining scale with agility, creativity with systems and energy with stability—but building such a relationship has executional complexities. We recall Tata Group's attempt to develop a supercomputer by working with a renowned mathematician of Mumbai. Some short-term dramatic results were achieved, but Tata and the innovator could not work together for long.

Nature teaches us that even a big herd of mighty elephants can be distracted and deranged by tiny bees which buzz around their flapping ears! Prof. Mohanbir Sawhney presented a paper titled 'How to Dance with Start-ups'[28] in 2018 at SP Jain Institute of Management and Research. He illustrated with examples of idiosyncratic international programmes: the Unilever Foundry Process, the Siemens Idea Contests, the G-Mill of General Mills, the start-up garage of BMW and the Bosch Chicago Connector. However, there were no examples from India.

Here is one: an Indian company called Galaxy Surfactants Ltd floated an initial public offering in the stock market. This company

---

[28] Mohanbir Sawhney, 'How to Dance with Start-ups', Smarter Balanced Assessment Consortium, 2018, https://www.spjimr.org/sbac-2018

was set up in the 1980s by two chemical engineers and two chartered accountants who had interned at Hindustan Unilever Ltd (HUL). They were bitten by the start-up bug in the 1980s. There was considerable encouragement from HUL. Personal care companies require very small quantities of several organic chemicals for the formulation of their products. To reduce import dependence for their customers, Galaxy reverse-engineered low-cost processes to deliver high quality at competitive costs. HUL could focus on formulation and consumer development. From this alliance, Galaxy grew—steadily and away from the public gaze. The company now boasts 1700 customers in India and overseas, listing every major personal care company. After the IPO, the market cap of the company may be around $1 billion. This is a terrific example of a start-up working with a large company by exploiting mutual strengths.

A dramatic American example: Cruise Automation is a San Francisco-based company, founded by serial entrepreneur Kyle Vogt. Kyle graduated in computer science from MIT (he did not drop out), founded Justin.tv, which he sold to Autodesk, founded Twitch, which he sold to Amazon, and in October 2013, he founded Cruise. He sold to General Motors (GM) for $1 billion in 2016. GM and Cruise faced many difficulties as they learnt to work together. Last month, General Motors unveiled GM Cruise, a fourth-generation vehicle, following their third-generation Chevy Bolt. Now that is progress, frenetic progress.

It took Galaxy Surfactants three decades to reach a market cap of $1 billion, but Cruise only three years. Surely it is different economies and different times, but it is worthwhile to study these cases.

The idea of small and big Indian companies collaborating is not new.

Lessons on Uncertainties

The stories of the next frontier—how the East appeared to Europeans in the 1500s, and how California appeared to Americans in the late

1800s—are well documented. The start-up world in India appears similar, like the frontier for a new India. Every day we are fed with stories, told with breathless excitement: India has the third-largest number of start-ups in the world, India's entrepreneurial system is growing rapidly, foreign money from China, South Africa and America is betting on India, and finally, that start-ups will create the much-needed jobs in India. Some believe in this narrative and others think this is just hyped and purely poppycock! Can history guide us a bit through the maze?

During recent times, we have had several exposures to what appear to be revolutionary ideas. Arunachalam Muruganantham— 'Pad Man'—inventor of the inexpensive sanitary pad, has been at it for over fifteen years. In spite of having a proven product and business model, he refuses to let corporates take the idea into rapid adoption among consumers. Of the 300 million women who need the product, how many have been reached?

During the last few years, three brilliant youngsters have innovated with revolutionary ideas—young Nilay Kulkarni has worked on a life-saving innovation that prevents stampede and loss of lives at Kumbh Mela and Haj. Fourteen-year-old Harshvardhana Jhala has designed a drone to detect landmines and save soldiers' lives. He has got Rs 5 crore funding for further development. Fifteen-year-old Akash Manoj has designed a skin patch which can predict a heart attack six hours before it occurs by measuring a protein, FABP3, in the body. All three have rightly been lauded by VIPs. India can be proud of such young people innovating to solve real social problems.

The question we struggle with is: will these ever see the light of day as commercial unicorns? 'Pad Man' refuses, the other three have a long way to go. Every interviewer applauds their innate qualities as genius and brilliant. Children who are declared to be geniuses in a family from the get-go, fail to live up to expectations. We wish their work and efforts be applauded, rather than any inherent brilliance. Personal approbation is counterproductive.

In her book *Ruling the Waves: Cycles of Discovery, Chaos, and Wealth from the Compass to the Internet*, Harvard Business School's Professor Deborah L. Spar describes lessons from history.[29] She argues that there are four phases—innovation, commercialization, anarchy and finally, rules. During the first phase, there are no rules, and governments underestimate the role and impact of new technologies. During the second phase, young pioneers and pirates set forth to commercialize the innovation. The story of TCS, Infosys and Bharti some decades ago is illustrative of the path of pioneers. They operated above the government who just did not understand how these companies worked, or what their customer offering was.

The current digital successors come through as the pirates; they smell the big money and they flock to the frontier, taking big risks, with foreign money. India's technology start-ups are now into the third phase of creative anarchy. Ownership in this phase is less important than speed; land grab and scale are more important than building customer value; raising capital is more important than profits, and entrepreneurs kill to grow on the premise that the winner takes all. Their mantra is valuations and exit, a bit like raising a child for adoption—for a price—it is completely mercenary.

Indian technology start-ups are hovering around, or are into the fourth phase now. They now seek government rules to prevent the unfair players who deploy foreign money to fight a battle on unlevel grounds. That is the OLA's grouse against Uber, of Paytm against Facebook's WhatsApp, and of Flipkart against Amazon. Furthermore, VCs with foreign money wish to bypass taxes after every round of higher valuations and new funding. The merits of their arguments are not our subject of commentary, but their behavioural pattern is. It suggests that the phase of welcoming regulation and government intervention, which is the fourth phase, has begun. The cycle of history repeats itself, not just in India, but globally. There are deep societal worries about the stranglehold of Google, Facebook and Apple in the

---

[29] Deborah L. Spars, *Ruling the Waves*, Houghton Mifflin Harcourt, 2001.

world, as well as Baidu, Alibaba and Tencent who are spreading out radially from dominance in China.

It is interesting to note that even 'successful' pirates received political patronage during historical times. Sir Francis Drake, the pirate of the seas, received special patronage from Queen Elizabeth I, while more recently, Rupert Murdoch received the special patronage of Margaret Thatcher.

Skills of Critical Thinking

Being aware of other stories and being sensitive to the changing landscape is only one part of the entrepreneur's cognitive awakening. The other part, and in some ways the more important part, is about how to think through the issues relevant to the opportunity. When faced with choosing between option A and option B, critical thinkers ask, 'Why not option C or option D?' Analysis of a problem requires delving deep into it. Another view can arise out of considering what landscape the problem is a part of. Such an approach or critical thinking helps generate new options.

It goes without saying that the ideas put forth here are of course not ultimate or all-pervasive and we all need to constantly evolve and learn. A lot of what we have posited here may become redundant or outdated before this book is even out in print. However, we hope that the reader still stands to benefit from the ways of our analysis and if nothing, hopefully, we have triggered off a healthy debate and discussion on the subject.

4

Look before You Leap

In this chapter, we have tried to demonstrate how intuitive optimism and scepticism enjoy a permanent quarrel with each other. How can entrepreneurs deal with these opposing thoughts? We express a view on a few verticals that appear to present entrepreneurial opportunities. By including our perspectives on the subject issues here, we merely seek to demonstrate the power of questioning that entrepreneurs must subject their ideas to. Our views are expressed as our opinions.

The Nature of Capital

As inequality increased in the world over the last several decades, a small percentage of people became hugely rich. They wished to deploy their wealth in high-return investments and were prepared to take bigger risks. This is the phenomenon that triggered the venture capital business—lots of capital and hunger for high-risk, high-return investment. In this process, start-ups—at least those who could pitch their ideas persuasively—could raise funds, based on the promise of exceptional growth and smart technology. However, in this game, the losers would outnumber the winners by a factor of 50:1.

For those who won, it surely became a great narrative. But what about the losers?

Every loser's tale is unique. The one thing all losers experience is a funder who pushed the entrepreneur to spend big money behind growth and market share. We recall the economist Milton Friedman's view about four types of money:

- Your money spent on others: spend the least and don't show hurry or generosity.
- Your money spent on yourself: get best value for the money spent.
- Other people's money spent on yourself: splurge as much as you can, like the company expense account.
- Others people's money spent on others: spend with gay abandon.

Entrepreneurs got used to spending 'other people's money on other people'. This phenomenon was the opposite of the wisdom gleaned from long-lasting companies. Our comments in this chapter originate from this dilemma.

Financial Prudence

On matters of finance, we believe that all organizations should proceed with some degree of prudence. Prior to the advent of technology start-ups, and from time immemorial, money was one of the factors of production that was always in short supply. Incidentally, it is our view that it continues to be so even today, however much media reports might make it sound otherwise. Then came the technology start-ups, and Silicon Valley VCs often believed that those who were 'first to market' got significant market shares, provided enormous amount of funds were made available. We are at a stage where this 'enormous' amount has hit an all-time high, leading us to infer that a bubble might burst shortly. But more troubling is the kind of culture that permeates the organization when you chase market share at virtually any cost.

Think of a situation where you are marooned on an island and have not eaten for days. When you get some food, it is most likely that you would end up overeating. Well, the same thing applies to availability of excess of money in an organization. But the long-term effects could be even more harmful. In an organization where executives are encouraged to spend recklessly, and at the same time fetch results, the cultural sensitivity to the value of money is likely to deteriorate and accountability may suffer, not to ignore the many distortions that might take place in execution. The interaction that takes place with the customer will also become increasingly transactional. It will be well worth to pause and assess whether market share acquisition is sustainable.

When one player in the vertical commences a hustle for market share, others who can afford to do so have no option but to follow suit. Invariably, the enticement for market share acquisition is monetary. You have any number of examples in India today.

Paytm Mall came into the e-commerce business belatedly. They must have wanted to enter the e-commerce market and make sure that Paytm (the payment mechanism) is used for the interaction. So the burn is now allocated across Paytm Mall and Paytm payments. It seems like an acceptable strategy on paper. It seems like killing two birds with one stone.

But will Paytm Mall or the payment mechanism ever be able to coexist without such heavy expenditure on discounts and giveaways? Will the marketing profession train the company to become discount maniacs? Will the organization's dependence on discounting become a habit? Will the competition in the industry be forced to adopt similar methods and will consumers become habituated to discounts?

Lower Price Is Not Always Good for the Consumer

All these fears and more are being reflected in the e-commerce world today. And there is more to it. Apart from distorting the e-commerce space, the impact of this discounting can be felt in the old-world retail economy that has been servicing the customer for years. Consumer-durable traders are distraught at the prices being offered online, which customers research before making a demand. Rentals in main markets kept pace with the retail growth. Now the old-world retailers are saddled with high rental overheads, and are finding it difficult to compete and offer comparable margins. But when they move out or close down, consumers are the ones who will suffer the most. Your neighbourhood grocer is under threat, as is your neighbourhood pharmacist. Lower prices do not always mean that the customer will benefit.

Just as we thought that the new-world taxi services have added value to our lives, for those of you who are regular travellers, you may have observed that cab rides are nearly 35–40 per cent more expensive than they were six months ago. And do we sense a higher fare on iPhones as compared to Android phones? And do we pay a higher price for things than a local resident when we go to a new town? The rules for customized offerings have a positive and a negative side to it. Does Amazon offer the same product at different prices on different days on the same website? Does an ad magically appear on the website to justify the higher price or lower offer? The changes that are rapidly taking place under the guise of analytics and technology are concerning. One possible outcome of this could be a fight to the finish, and the 'last' man standing could only be one or two players. A situation which telecom in India is close to attaining. And once that happens, we may see an inexorable price increase.

Digital Divide by Language

The Internet operates mostly in English. For decades, consumer-marketing professionals have targeted the easily reachable urban, English-speaking customer. And then gradually they have moved to the vernacular audience who also have purchasing power. From the language to the layout and navigation, there is a yawning gap between the customers who receive information in the vernacular language versus those receiving it in English.

RedSeer Management Consulting has captured this reality with the broad classification of just fifty million individuals called 'English first' followed by 200 million individuals who fall into the 'vernacular first' category. And that pretty much summarizes the purchasing class in India. So, it is worthwhile for entrepreneurs to bear this digital divide in mind when targeting offerings for the Indian market. India has roughly about 500 million Internet users. This is also driven by social media apps like TikTok. Advertising and reaching the TikTok-consuming population will call for a totally different skill set and approach.

Valuations and More

It was reported that Swiggy had raised $1 billion at a valuation of some $3.3 billion. The year 2018 also saw the valuation of edtech firm Byju's at $4.5 billion, and a number of other astonishing valuations that have catapulted the investors' and promoters' net worth into the millions or billions of dollars. And it would be interesting to understand how a company like Swiggy, which is still burning money every month, is able to continuously raise money and at increasingly higher valuations. To understand this, we have to go back to what we call the 'Silicon Valley Way' and the mindset of market-making investors in Silicon Valley.

Firstly, the Silicon Valley pundits must like this vertical. Food tech (food delivery is for some mysterious reason, referred to as food tech!) is yet to make money anywhere in the world. If the data capture is wide, and Silicon Valley believes that data is the new oil, then the particular vertical would qualify. So, is the VC community in Silicon Valley funding start-ups in this space? To what extent have these start-ups established that they are able to accumulate data?

Secondly, there should be adequate room for a price increase in a near monopolistic (or duopolistic) market justifying the heavily subsidized entry and sustained losses that the new entrant to the market would make. The strategy then becomes one of the biggest in the market, and it is popularly believed in the technology-investing world that 'first to market' is very important. And with enormous amount of data in your repository, you can raise barriers to entry that a newbie and the competition will find difficult to emulate or overcome. Third and of course of no less importance is the quality of the entrepreneur that is seeking to enter this market.

Remember that the market makers are keen to enter this market as quickly as possible and have a vested interest in raising the stakes. They now need to identify entrepreneurs who have the vision and the passion to execute. If it is thumbs-up on these parameters, then the market makers are ready to roll and they provide some money to get started, make sure that the execution does indeed happen and then are willing to put in large sums of money to accelerate the entire process. And that is what one sees sometimes when it comes to valuation.

They now have to find a balance between the actual valuation of the company and ensuring that the promoters have enough skin in the game, to be interested enough to toil for the next few years until big numbers are achieved. And as the valuation increases, it is an invitation to other investors to join the party and come in with smaller or larger investments. As the size of the party increases (meaning more and more interested investors come in), the valuation increases rapidly and the promoter comes under increasing pressure to execute faster, so that it becomes possible to show the new prospective investors that capital is the key factor of production that is standing in the way of a promising deal. In the case of Swiggy, for instance, the story would have been so profound that Naspers may put in $1 billion for a 30 per cent holding in Swiggy (formal confirmation of $1 billion and $3.3 billion is awaited at the time of writing).

The mistake that new entrepreneurs can make is that they actually begin to believe that their company is actually worth billions. Market makers have created the conditions for the new investor to believe that there is enough headroom for much bigger valuations to follow.

India's first generation of unicorns adopted business models from the US. Ride-hailing company Ola is similar to Uber, for example. Flipkart is similar to Amazon. Paytm is similar to Alipay. But a new group of companies addressing the Indian market is clearly also on the move forward. Byju's addresses the tuition market in India where the pressure on academic results is immense. Policy Bazaar offers online insurance and facilitates comparison shopping. Both enjoy the status of being a unicorn, and the business model is adapted to the local conditions and does not rely on Silicon Valley comparisons. In addition, there has been visible movement in B2B offerings which target the US market out of India.

Although the SaaS business model is known in Silicon Valley, Freshworks works its way bottom-up. Udaan connects more than 1,50,000 buyers and sellers of electronics, clothing and staples, and offers a total solution in a market where logistics and supply chains are less organized. Oyo Hotels and Homes, valued at around $5 billion, is pushing hotel owners to upgrade poorly equipped lodges, to include better facilities and list them on Oyo's website. As we write this, it has been reported that Oyo funded by Softbank is making rapid progress in China with a model not too dissimilar than India's. There is also news of the developments at Oyo's key funder, Softbank, and that can have a big effect on Oyo and its future! But managing a customer-facing business across geographies is not something that a start-up can easily digest.

In a sense therefore, optimistic and intrepid entrepreneurs can identify a local gap in the system and use technology to bridge this gap either in the area of supply chain or quality or efficiency. Oyo is spreading its wings like an albatross to enter the shared living space. We also read that WeWork dropped its plan to make a public offering,[1] largely because the pre-money valuation was found to be too high,

---

[1] Marie C. Baca, 'WeWork Says It Will Withdraw Its Initial Public Offering Filing, Postponing IPO Indefinitely', *Washington Post*, 2 October 2019, https://www.washingtonpost.com/technology/2019/09/30/wework-says-it-will-withdraw-its-initial-public-offering-filing/

first at \$47 billion, then \$28 billion and finally below \$15 billion. WeWork's founder resigned in the subsequent scandal that emerged. Oyo has emerged as the highest valued unicorn out of India and is poised for a fund raise of \$1.5 billion on a valuation of \$18 billion. These are heady times but an acid test awaits. For a person already managing a diverse, multi-location company, adding a chain of hotels to the mix does seem like a long shot. The hospitality business requires a level of experience and an eye for detail that Oyo is yet to display.

In summary, if you are driven by a desire to create a unicorn, there is nothing wrong. But keep your head on your shoulders as you begin to fill a genuine gap in the marketplace and seek to deliver what organizations have been seeking to deliver since time immemorial—namely profits. During this process, if you become a millionaire or a billionaire, we wish you good luck. But you will finally be evaluated by the value you bring to the value chain that you have identified, and you will finally be judged by your ability to monetize the same.

All valuations in the start-up world value a company based on what they think the company would command in the future. So, you need to capture the imagination of the investor at each stage and convince them that there is huge upside. This holds good irrespective of whether you are seeking to obtain a valuation of Rs 10 crore or \$10 billion. The only difference is that as you grow and become stock market eligible, the stock market will determine what your value is and will be. We already hear murmurs from the media that Silicon Valley has firmed up its new mantra: 'the road to profitability' is now being unabashedly muttered in sublime circles. The Softbank Vision Fund 2 appears to be floundering in its fundraise. And the world is on the verge of a recession as the US and China spar. Are we on the verge of a meltdown with regard to unicorns?

Trust

How is it that we hear about an apparent improvement in the ease of doing business in India, yet we do not feel it on a day-to-day basis?

This essentially boils down to a breakdown of trust, law and order which occurs somewhere or the other every day. What happens as a result is that all matters (for example, business, trading and new investments) slow down around us. Distrust imposes a tremendous burden on society and when this happens, speeding up things and making up for this slowdown calls for additional energy all around. Starting with entrepreneurial activity. It might be pertinent to also examine the ecosystem in which all businesses in India operate.

1. Section 56 of the Income Tax Act was introduced by the UPA government; it was ostensibly aimed at ensuring that money laundering be curbed. This later got translated by the income tax authorities as an 'angel' tax wherein all start-ups that were raising funds at valuations higher than the book value of the company would be subject to scrutiny and liable to income tax for the difference between book value and actual valuation. In a country where funds for small business continue to be in short supply, this announcement was met with incredulity by the start-up community. That still did not stop the IT authorities from picking on a few start-ups and issuing demand notices. Now, instead of paying attention to their business, promotors were required to provide information and data on the book value of their business a few years ago, and explain the circumstances under which they managed to raise funds at higher valuations.

   Of course, there were amendments made, wherein the affidavit of a chartered accountant was deemed sufficient if a discounted cash flow (DCF) method was to be used. By the time the NDA government came to power, this was slowly becoming a major issue. Did matters improve after the NDA government came to power? Truth be told, matters only got worse. IT officers kept sending demand notices to hundreds of start-ups all over the country. Ministers and representatives of the Department for Promotion of Industry and Internal Trade (DPIIT) kept saying that this would be amended but the notices kept coming. In stray instances, the income tax authorities froze the bank accounts and helped themselves to funds on an ad hoc basis. Start-ups were left running around converting funds to inaccessible assets.

This confusion and chaos resulting from the government's lack of empathy is a classic example of a breakdown in trust. A lack of coordination between the government and government-nominated departments effectively emasculates the government itself. Leave alone the long-suffering citizens, entrepreneurs in the developing world face this all the time. What is the effort-to-value ratio? Some calculations place the ratio at 40:1 in India compared to 1:1 in the US. We do not have immediate access to a similar figure for China, but it would possibly be 10:1. This is just to set the context for consultants and start-ups as to what they can expect out of India. Mere presence of 1.3 billion people does not mean that the market will naturally emerge and we will be able to tap into it. What would take ten years in China may well take twenty-five years to achieve in India, if not more.

2. When things are difficult, one retreats to the familiar and the previously tried. For example, building an app or starting an enterprise is not the same in Bangalore as it is in Beijing or sitting in a dorm at Harvard (where the Facebook app originated). Consider the recently announced e-commerce policy that appears to penalize multinational companies. The ink on the Walmart deal with Flipkart had barely dried when this new e-commerce policy that seems to work against the interest of the two prevailing multinationals, who have committed billions of dollars to their investment in India, was announced. It is clear that decision-makers are totally distanced from reality in India.

3. It isn't that no businesses in India have been able to overcome the trust deficit. Amul came into a milk shortage situation and through the mobilization of cooperatives, and despite the

constant meddling of the state and central governments, India is the largest producer of milk in the world today. No doubt there are exceptions, even from India, but for the rest, waiting for somebody else to bell the cat is not going to work. This trust must be built up by the enterprise, and there is little doubt that it will be an uphill task and that building such trust will take a long time.

4. If you have a dispute that goes into litigation, how long before this comes up in court? And how long before this is concluded? The harsh reality is that nobody has any idea and we retreat into our businesses with the belief that the justice system will take forever, and we plan accordingly. This is why one often finds tenants in dispute with the landlords openly admitting that they have no intention of vacating their rented flats, since any legal decision of eviction would take so long that the landlord would be happy to pay to see them go. We have a delayed and unpredictable justice system. The large majority of businesses in India have to operate within the thirty-year waiting period to obtain justice. Both complainant and offender know this and act accordingly. We expect our politicians to layer their own bread with butter obtained illicitly. Corruption is rampant. In such an atmosphere, we do not know whom to trust. Similarly, businesses aren't divorced from their socio-economic and cultural setting, and do get affected from this inherent lack of trust.

5. It is important that we set our expectations right and be aware of the environment we inhabit. Especially if we're trying to achieve what China has seemingly achieved in a very short period. The narrow middle class in terms of numbers, the low Internet penetration rate, the trust deficit—all these factors in India collectively slow us down as we claw our way forward. Despite all the efforts being made to overcome these difficulties, we should be prepared to wait before we see results for our efforts.

About Hypes and Hype Cycles

The current flavour of the season when it comes to technology is artificial intelligence (AI) and the huge impact that it is going to have on jobs and of course on mankind. The reality is that where AI stands today, it is currently being overhyped. Don't forget that thirty years ago, the biggest fear of trade unions worldwide was the computer. Unions worldwide resisted the introduction of the computer since they feared that jobs of their members would be lost. At the time, the majority of the members of trade unions were blue-collar and low-level white-collar workers. In hindsight, we know that this reaction was exaggerated and if anything, productivity went up and more jobs were created than lost.

AI threatens to do what the computer never did. But that does not mean that there is no hype in the brilliant tales that are emerging as to what AI will achieve. Our own take on this is to carefully follow companies like Amazon and what they are achieving. Amazon has pretty much been a leader in labour-saving devices, be it on the warehouse floor or elsewhere. With a farsighted approach, building its carefully cultivated image as a technology company of the future, Amazon is pioneering the delivery of e-commerce goods using drones. And it is not impossible to visualize that this may very well happen someday. The real question is, how far is that someday?

Moreover, the reason why we tend to reject these farfetched ideas is that we think of these matters as a zero-sum game. We think of e-commerce delivery through drones replacing some two million delivery persons across the nation in the year 2025. And this is where technology fools us. It promises to make tomorrow happen today, and makes it sound so simple that we are tempted to believe the time framework that they promise. To more than 50 per cent of the human population, such an eventuality in the year 2050 is of little interest beyond academic. And to be able to fund R&D and raise money from investors, there has to be an element of urgency and a sense that it is imminent. It is against this background of the generic nature of technology news that we present our views and personal opinions on nearly a dozen online business platforms. However, AI impact on fields like health care, finance and law enforcement is expected to be delayed. This is partially due to lack of accuracy and partially due to regulatory bodies seeking to intercept the likely discrimination that might follow. Here are a few illustrations:

In the field of health care, the data might suggest a high probability of the onset of chronic illness. Health professionals are yet to determine how they would deal with probabilistic outcomes. The fact that one may have a 70 per cent probability of a cancer diagnosis in a particular organ cannot mean that you remove a limb or an organ today when there is no clear evidence of such an onset. At best, you could be more watchful and new tests might emerge that would catch the evidence even earlier.

Is there an opportunity for a new company here? The answer is yes and no! There is no doubt that e-commerce has been heavily subsidized by capital. And there is even less doubt that two of the heavyweights in the world are both firmly lodged in the Indian market.

Yet, it is also true that the market for e-commerce has been built based on 'lower prices'. Conventional marketing wisdom tells us that brands are not built based on lower prices unless it is an intentional positioning, and it is done for the seeking of volumes. The dollar store in the US is one such example. However, when the market is being built based on factors other than price, then the sustainability of a brand built on product discounts becomes another matter altogether. Both Amazon and Walmart are global brands, and surely bring value to the table that goes beyond discounting. Close on their heels are Snapdeal and Paytm. Both have been attempting to capture market share by making deeply discounted offers. Certainly three of them, if not all four of them, have enough capital to take a ten-year outlook on the market.

And last but not least, it is rumoured that Google is likely to enter the e-commerce space in India.[2]

We also know that Reliance has clear intentions of asserting itself in the offline and online e-commerce market in India. That makes for yet another deep-pocketed entrant. Continued discount wars are inimical for all concerned, and will inevitably become an occasional practice and more brand-led (as it used to be before e-commerce came into being). That of course became an issue for privately labelled brands, which may find it difficult to compete for customer mind-space through conventional media. But as it happens, conventional media itself may be in the process of intermediation and may take a different form. Let us briefly explore this last statement to better understand the overall space of e-commerce.

E-commerce players have already realized that the initial phase of early adopters is somewhat over. And they appear to be aware that the discounting-to-attract-customer phase has also run its course. Visible action is now becoming increasingly apparent. Our thesis is based on several major assumptions:

- Google's proposed entry into e-commerce is a signal that the existing business model of advertising is now under threat.
- Amazon has already asserted itself as a player in the online advertising business.
- E-commerce players across the board have somewhat understood that discounting is not a sustainable marketing strategy.
- Consumers are increasingly using the mobile phone to use the Internet, and this will continue to be the case. E-commerce will be no exception.

---

[2] Shreya Ganguly, 'Google All Set to Enter Ecommerce Space In India with Its Online Storefront', Inc42.com, 11 October 2018, https://inc42.com/buzz/google-all-set-to-enter-ecommerce-space-in-india-with-its-online-storefront/

- Early adopters of e-commerce have already entered the market and the 100 million or so entrants seem to represent a significant purchasing power. New customers will continue to arrive, but will require more customized offerings to be attracted. AI-driven data analytics will come to the fore and new entrants will be discouraged from entering a market where data gathering is a formidable task ahead of them.

- For data to become more vibrant and rich, customer engagement must first and foremost become more sophisticated and immersive. That would make customized offerings more valuable.

A larger profile of customer habits can aid the creation of customized offerings. This alone is a good reason for e-commerce players to move into related offerings which until now represented independent verticals.

For instance, Paytm's early entry into travel and hospitality now becomes more explicable. Or for that matter, their entry into e-commerce through Paytm Mall. As we see today, Amazon has already announced its proposed entry into travel and hospitality. Data that until recently showed a profile of purchases made and the brands purchased, to be viewed perhaps alongside demographics, now becomes data further sliced by travel and hospitality habits of customers. The goal of e-commerce is obviously to 'travel' with the customer and make customized offerings to you on your mobile, which incidentally is the easiest way to travel with you. In a world where all data is available to your e-commerce vendor, it is easier for him to offer you deals to purchase wherever you are, whenever you desire! How long before e-commerce vendors enter the food delivery business, and once they know your travel plans, they should be able to offer you the food of your preferences in another city best matched to the orders you placed in the past in your home town.

Does it sound like something George Orwell would have imagined? Would we view this as an invasion of our privacy? Or would the world soon be marching to the tune of 'Retail Commerce Good, E-commerce Better'?

But before we depart from the subject of e-commerce, let us also understand where entertainment is headed and what our consumption patterns will be for the same in the future.

Firstly, entertainment is already being received through a variety of devices and is available whenever you want it. As consumer traffic increasingly moves to the mobile phone, the kind of entertainment that we would want to consume might also undergo some changes. For instance, it is likely that the long-format movie that we viewed in the cinema hall will gradually give way to a format of fifteen-minute stories or short films—in just the same way that cricket got truncated from five-day test matches to a T20 format. Movies seek to entertain, and as we spend more of our waking hours on mobile phones, we are always pressed for time. Just like the T20 enabled us consume our desired dose of cricket in a few hours, instead of five days, it is logical that we would seek to obtain our dose of escapist entertainment in fifteen minutes and perhaps many times a day, instead of in a few hours once a fortnight.

For a while, broadcast TV filled this gap. It gave us entertainment at a greater frequency as we spent an increasing number of hours on the TV; the three-hour film format changed to twenty-minute serials that began to occupy the bulk of our daily entertainment consumption. The broadcaster was still determining when we could consume this entertainment. Netflix was the first to break this barrier and offer a multi-serial show that was available for viewing whenever you want and for however long at a time you wanted to watch. You no longer had to wait another week to discover what happened next in your serialized show. And with entertainment moving from the cinema halls to the TV set and now on to the laptop or mobile, advertising too moved alongside.

That is perhaps why Google needs to move into a greater participation in the action on the mobile. Google is already there on the mobile when we consume ultra-short format entertainment as on

YouTube, ByteDance or TikTok, etc. Consumers too are creating their own channels here. Institutional entry into this sector will go alongside the retail generation of user-defined content. And there is competitive pressure across genres, and the ultimate marketplace competes for the time of the consumer. Whether short or long format, it has implications for the institutional producers of content, the cinema halls, the broadcast channels and the advertisers who used the eyeball count to generate revenues. And foremost among them is Google.

At the supply end, the production houses in Hollywood have enormous assets, locking up capital and determining indirectly the final pricing of the movies. Movie stars have captured a major portion of the value chain.

As the short format comes into being and retail producers pop up at the lower-cost end of production, all producers will feel the impact. And so will the rest of the value chain. Independent producers of the long format will find that the cost of failing has tremendously increased. No longer does the distribution channel, which has a monopoly on exhibition for at least six weeks, find that the monopoly can be retained. In fact, the short format may not even lend itself for exhibition in the cinema halls. And we then come to the traditional broadcasters such as Zee TV, HBO and Star Movies, and they find that the risks associated with purchase of rights to screen are no longer following the rules of the past. Prices of content will start sliding as low-cost content from independent producers becomes increasingly available, and the skill set required to assess this content will need to be discovered. Against this background, advertising will most likely migrate to that channel that assures visibility of a specific target audience. The bygone days of click farms have made way for the e-commerce players. They will build subscription revenue and treat entertainment as yet another product that they offer. Cross tabulated and filtered against the spending habits of customers that they already possess, e-commerce becomes the most efficient method of delivering advertising over the Internet. And the adoption that Amazon has for its keyword advertising is an early indicator.

Eventually of course, all the e-commerce players will seek to introduce entertainment content and will once again compete against each other. For the consumer, however, as it magically happened in the case of broadcast TV, movie entertainment may also become free. And it will be delivered on device of choice and consumer can consume the content when so desired and in a continuous manner across devices. And the most accurate delivery of content to the right target audience will take place when there is e-commerce data at the background to enable filtering and pinpointing of target audience. Special effects movies will be few and far between and these will be designed for the big screen and the movie theatres will once again have to gear their acoustics to face the new challenges. But here we have bad news for the consumers. The cost of viewing these movies in the movie theatre will rise. But wait, there is good news too. Virtual and augmented reality with haptics (the science of applying physical touch to interact with computer applications) will now have a venue and audience. As access to entertainment comes increasingly to mobile devices, the clash will be for consumers' time, which is already under siege. We can expect the verticals within entertainment to clash for a time slot that could either be allocated to a mobile game or to a short film.

So one must enter this market with this knowledge in hand. In addition, you can reasonably expect at least a couple of more deep-pocketed new entrants to make an assault on the Indian e-commerce market over the next ten years.

Even today, roughly 90 per cent of all retail trade comes from the organized sector, and arguably some fifteen million retail outlets exist in India. McKinsey from Mckinsey and Co. famously forecasted in the early '90s, that organized retail in the form of modern trade, which accounted for 2–3 per cent of retail business, would eventually become, by the year 2000, some 20 per cent of retail trade. Even by 2019, modern trade accounts formed a mere

8 per cent of all retail trade in India. E-commerce was a mere 12 per cent of all retail trade.[3]

But these statistics are not the last word on where e-commerce is headed. Even as we work on this book, the government has announced its latest policy on e-commerce—substantially placing foreign e-commerce players at some disadvantages. We will not go into the pros and cons of the policy and its implications just yet. The policy has very recently been enunciated and is most likely to undergo several changes. But it is interesting to see that both Amazon and Walmart follow a hybrid model of conventional retail and e-tail. As both of them get a better feel of the consumer in tier-2 and -3 towns, the model will yet again undergo changes.

What is evident is that several online categories have adopted a hybrid model during the expansion stage, Lenskart and Myntra being good examples. Several marketplace makers also have a medium-to-long term interest in offering private label brands of their own, wherein they hope to make the kind of margins that a brand owner makes. That means that the marketplace model allows for the distribution of private labels belonging to the marketplace alongside the availability of other brands. In simple terms, it may be in the interest of governments to regulate marketplaces. If you are at a retail store and offer brands of several companies of a particular product category, and eventually you begin to offer your own label of product alongside, there is scope for conflict of interest.

Conventional wisdom suggests that this effectively means that marketplace brands compete with the brands belonging to their own distribution partners, arguably creating conditions for conflict of interest. Such an arrangement might be short-lived in nature and perhaps even detrimental to the long-term peaceful coexistence in the marketplace. Ola had introduced company-owned vehicles alongside their partner taxis which were independently owned. Although there

---

[3]   IndiaRetailing.com, https://shop.indiaretailing.com/product/images-retail-february-2011/

may have been no actual preferential treatment, the independent taxi owners were strongly of the opinion that such was indeed the case. In our opinion, this kind of conflict of interest, wherein an organization competes with its own partners, is inimical (and non-Ayruvedic too; more on this later) to long-term existence.

Headwinds and Tailwinds

The abrupt way the government announced its new e-commerce policy does not augur well for the industry or for the ease of doing business in India. Walmart–Flipkart and Amazon had committed themselves to the Indian market with substantial investments. These new policy announcements should have been indicated to them in advance. There is also a hint of the rules favouring an Indian major. That is like going back to the license-raj regime. One needs to tread carefully before entering an industry where government policies keep changing frequently.

The government is also trying to provide an environment that encourages start-ups. It is therefore in the interest of every start-up to register itself with the DIPP and make sure that they are uniquely placed to take full advantage of whatever incentives the government may provide in the future.

Finally, and lest we should paint too optimistic an outlook, we are experiencing a worldwide recession, thanks to the COVID-19 crisis. It has surely taken all of us by surprise. India and China were meant to hold up the rest of the world in the event of a recession. Both countries now appear to be having their own individual problems, and growth rates across the globe are at a low ebb. The new-age industries have not experienced a recession of a worldwide kind. And this unexpected upheaval can send the best of plans for a toss. E-commerce in India has not yet faced a recession, and the jury is still out on this possibility.

SECTION 2

Grown-ups

5

The Importance of a Long Life

Human beings have always sought the secret to a long and content life—the idea of *ikigai* in Japan, *hygge* in Denmark, and *longue durée* in France. Each culture has figured out its own formulae for extending human life and one finds that there are many commonalities.

In India, the word 'Ayurveda' literally means the science of long life. We shall discuss this concept in more detail later in the book. The term 'Corporate Ayurveda' in the title may appear mysterious— Corporate and Ayurveda are not natural allies! The mystery is unnecessary as we have tried to establish a simple connection: just as Ayurveda has distilled lessons on good health and long life, 'Corporate Ayurveda' is about the lessons and the wisdom from long-life companies for future start-ups.

Entrepreneurship and business, conducted through legal entities called companies, are the engines of economic growth and job creation in any society. Start-ups and grown-ups are of great importance to society and the nation. Great companies are institutions, founded and designed to enjoy a long life. Unilever, Tata, IBM, Nestlé, Dabur and such institutions carry images, folklore and history. Such companies have discovered distinctive methods to ensure for themselves a long life because there is no single formula for creating a long-life company.

The general lessons from grown-up companies across cultures must hold some wisdom for today's start-up founders to create potentially long-living companies.

Corporate Ayurveda

Ayurveda literally means the science of life. It represents the oldest Indian system of medicines and healthy lifestyle principles. According to ancient texts dating back to the first millennium, Ayurveda is a holistic approach to healing. It strives to understand the core or root of the problem rather than just visible symptoms. Ayurveda is synonymous with a long healthy life.

According to Ayurveda, the human body is perceived as an inter-related complex of energy. When these three elements strike a balance and are in harmony, there is good health. When they are imbalanced, weaknesses develop. These three elements that essentially run the human body are wind, bile and phlegm. Wind refers to the gases/fluids of the digestive system, bile refers to the thick secretion from the liver, and phlegm refers to the thick secretion from the throat. In allegorical terms, these three manifest as the forces of the universe or as *energies*, the force of the *mind* and the force of the *soul*. These three forces tend to get out of balance due to the habits and lifestyle of the individual—for example, eating the wrong foods at wrong times or overburdening the liver with certain unhealthy beverages and diets. Other important factors are inherited genes, improper lifestyle, negative thinking and poor emotional balance. It is very important for these three forces to be balanced for the body and mind to be healthy.

In a similar way, a society remains healthy when the three forces of economy, education and eudemonia are in harmony and balance.

Using the same principle, nations and societies must also maintain a balance. This balance pertains to the three E's—economy, education and eudemonia.

Economy refers to the organizations and institutions, the entrepreneurial and business activities that generate jobs, income and prosperity. Economy provides the jobs for people to earn a living, and by extension, the necessary energy for a society to sustain itself.

Education refers to the development of the human mind in a society. It refers to not only formal education but also to a larger and deeper understanding and appreciation of life and people around you. Such a wholesome education leads to not just mental, intellectual growth but social and cultural development of society as well.

Eudemonia refers to good health and a broader sense of well-being such as happiness, contentedness and optimism about the future. This is akin to the well-being of the soul in the body.

Societies and nations that have achieved a balance among their economy, education and eudemonia have a good chance of enjoying a long healthy life. This is evidenced by the lessons of history from the great empires of the world—Persian, Roman, Greek, Ming, Ottoman, Mughal—all of them can be adduced as examples. The pattern conforms to the secret of Ayurveda as applied to the human body.

The West too seems to endorse the native wisdom of Ayurveda, albeit parts of it. They lend to it a more modern experimental rigour. In the field of evolutionary biology, it is said quite frequently that the absence of evidence is not evidence of absence.[1]

The Business Builder's Mindset

There are good practices for building great companies and institutions. The concept of a 'builder' is interesting in this context.[2]

In professional or social set-ups, people often ask each other what they do or where they work. Imagine if people begin asking what

---

[1]   Lawrence I. Bonchek, 'Absence of Evidence Is Not Evidence of Absence', *Journal of Lancaster General Health* 11, No. 2, 2016, http://www.jlgh.org/JLGH/media/Journal-LGH-Media-Library/Past%20Issues/Volume%2011%20-%20Issue%203/Editors-Desk-Absence-of-Evidence

[2]   Jim Clifton and Sangeeta Badal, *Born to Build*, Gallup, 2018.

other people are *building*. It would surely be an unusual question and people may struggle for an answer.

A business 'builder' is a creator of economic energy in a place where none existed before. Builders create a demand for a product or service where there was no demand in the first place. A builder combines three characteristics:

- Creates something that did not exist before, like a rainmaker.
- Acts as a preserver and conductor bringing order to the forces, like a conductor.
- Brings cutting expertise into action, like a subject expert.

The three—the rainmaker, the conductor and the expert—must come together for an entrepreneur to build something new.

Innovative ideas, new technologies, and the birth and growth of start-ups—all of these are at the core of economic growth. The economic history of business growth is well known. The transformative role of the Industrial Revolution, followed by the electrical, automotive, silicon and digital revolutions, is seared into the minds of experts and the general public alike.

The inexorable truth for India, or indeed for any nation, is that job creation and economic growth in the future depend crucially on the population succeeding with and doing new things—not just IT start-ups, but start-ups on a much broader basis. Rarely in history has the future of a nation depended on its youth as much as the future of the youth depended on the nation's propensity to allow them to be enterprising, as it did in the Indian context. It will either be a demographic dividend or a demographic disaster.

In this book, the focus is on entrepreneur-led new ventures, which is what most readers would understand by the word 'start-up'. However, the authors feel that the term 'start-up' is also a moniker for all entrepreneurial activities that energize and add value to the national economy. They are conducted in the private sector and the public sector, in large companies and in small companies; such risk-taking and innovative activities occur in laboratories, factories and marketplaces—all crucially important for a nation to progress.

Innovator and Entrepreneur

The terms 'innovator' and 'entrepreneur' are often used interchangeably. However, there is a difference that must be appreciated.

The *innovator* is the person with the idea. Every creative idea emanates from an innovator's curiosity and the need for experimentation. Without an idea, or an innovator, the process cannot even begin. It is a necessary thing, but is it sufficient? What else is required? Well, lots.

The *entrepreneur* is the person who builds a business model around the idea. The business model requires the entrepreneur to prepare and engage with a business plan and learn to create customers, find funds to undertake the risks associated with any new venture, and manage the company's plan of execution while simultaneously mitigating the risks. It is a complex process that can be sleep-depriving.

Many creative people assume that getting the idea is the key. Indian academics are being encouraged to take their ideas to the market. Many Indian scientists or academics have no clue about how to take an idea to the market. That is where the entrepreneur comes in. Coming up with innovative ideas is only a part of the key as can be seen from the points made above. Unlike the 1960s, in the present times, there is a lot of money being diverted to the innovation system—not just venture capital, but funds from government, high-net-worth individuals (HNIs), home offices and many more. This is positive but increases the burden on the entrepreneur.

Curiosity and Turbulence

Trends about the rise and fall of fortunes in business cause turbulence as well as curiosity in the minds of every generation. Current trends in corporate longevity are contrary to those that existed fifty years ago. Companies with well-known names are being merged, or they just fail, or descend rapidly into trouble. Recent examples being Xerox, Lehman Brothers and Toys R Us.

Academics like Sydney Finkelstein and Jim Collins suggest that this happens because these companies could not foresee the evolution of consumer tastes and markets, or had become lazy and stuck in a rut, or had become boring places for young people to work at. The same phenomenon afflicts humans who cannot cope with change and therefore it is easy to see a parallel between a company and a human being.

Everywhere in the world, anything new is initially viewed with suspicion. If one were to observe innovations that challenged the existing order of things, over the last two centuries, one would find many were often associated with issues that may threaten the individual or the traditional structures of society: having an adverse effect on health, children disobeying parents, the breaking down of class distinctions, enabling increasing independence among women and other such 'ills'.

When the newly discovered form of the novel came around, the philologist William Jones is noted to have said that the reading of novels is to the mind what dram-drinking is to the body!

When new media forms came into existence, the pre-existing media had to struggle to compete.

People resisted the novel, television and new forms of music like rock and roll as much as many today resist e-books, social media and perhaps electronic music.

Challenge by the Young

Yet, humankind has progressed for sure, whichever period in time one might examine. It has never been a story of doom and gloom. This is so because the young challenge the old. Posing a challenge to the established beliefs is a good thing; indeed it is the essence of change and adaptability.

In India, we have a rich tradition of the young being the harbinger of change and evolution who challenge the norms. Here are two examples from our mythology: The fact that Sri Krishna told Arjuna in the Bhagavad Gita that he could only impart knowledge, and Arjuna must figure out himself how to use that knowledge to do what is right, suggests that the knowledge that is passed down from generation to generation is universal but its application is subjective and ever-evolving. In the Katha Upanishad, the young Nachiketa confronted Yama with issues relating to life after death, the soul, salvation and other such deep philosophical questions, which display the curiosity in the young to question, probe and understand traditional knowledge, which is how societies evolve and progress.

Relevant to the subject of this book, the relationship between the young company founders and the established business veterans would be interesting to explore within the context of the above discussion. There is a feverish excitement around the world about new companies and founders. The GAFA companies (Google, Amazon, Facebook and Apple) and their fabled founders have become global icons, just as the founders of MakeMyTrip and Naukri.com have become Indian icons. In 2013, when the founder of Cowboy Ventures, Aileen Lee, coined the expression 'unicorn' for start-ups with a billion-dollar valuation, she unwittingly unleashed a strong ambitious energy within the masses. At that time, India had no unicorns. Now, India has twenty-seven!

The Indian financial newspapers are going ballistic about start-ups, so too are venture capitalists and entrepreneurs. India is reported to be the third-largest country in the world in terms of the number of start-ups. Start-up craze seems to have caught the imagination of every yuppie in India, intoxicated by fables about creating incredible wealth in ridiculously short time periods, the beckoning of exciting and rapidly evolving technologies, the rise and fall of unicorns, the rags-to-riches stories of founders.

In short, there is great a sense of excitement, perhaps even hubris, about what start-ups can do and achieve. As it always happens, the explorers on start-up expeditions believe that they belong to the lucky minority, may be the 1–2 per cent, who will survive and make it to the top; they all believe that others will magically falter and fall on the long and perilous journey somehow, but not them.

Serious Indian commentators have opined that start-ups are the answer to resurgent economic growth and job creation. According to them, start-ups are the panacea for all problems of India. These are contentious views, especially for a nation like India.

How Should Grown-ups Share Their Wisdom with Start-ups?

What start-ups tend to do is thought to be so different from what grown-ups do. There is a well-established community of grown-up companies like Tata, Godrej and Unilever who have been and are continuing to do great things that truly matter without much fanfare—generating wealth for shareholders, launching new brands, setting up factories, paying taxes, creating employees who earn real money and adding to community prosperity. It is fashionable, though inaccurate, for people to view these well-established companies as dinosaurs awaiting their call to extinction. Some companies are indeed dinosaurs. However, many established companies are vigorously alive and young, fighting off the afflictions of age.

India needs grown-ups as well as start-ups, not one or the other. How can the wisdom of grown-ups be shared with start-ups, its next generation? How could grown-ups share the secrets of good health and long life with the start-ups?

We sat down over a cup of Nilgiri tea at Coonoor (Tamil Nadu) and posed each other many such questions. We quickly agreed that surely a preachy or moralistic tone ('when we were young . . .') is counterproductive. We decided instead to simply state some facts and perhaps draw some metaphors about maintaining youthfulness as one starts to mature and about what is important during the renewal of companies. We agreed that such and other significant information should be assembled and presented, leaving the reader to reflect on this knowledge and adopt what appealed to them in their own context.

Revolutionary or Evolutionary Change?

Do the threats that demand change occur to companies suddenly, sort of cataclysmically, or does the change occur gradually?

In America, some technology companies like the GAFAs, are approaching individual market values of one trillion US dollars. The traditional companies like General Motors (GM) and General Electric (GE) are trailing far behind.

Is it merely an evolutionary intergenerational change? Has evolution started to display its magic? Is it true that a new species of companies is emerging? Is business really undergoing a cataclysmic transition, something like the change from the Triassic to the Jurassic age? Is there a phenomenon which current players are unwilling or unable to see because they are too close to the change to have an objective view of the situation?

Cataclysmic change is thought to be dramatic and sudden, while evolutionary change bears only the seed of a dramatic change, but embedded in the gentler cycle of evolutionary waves.

The world of business has its own experience of evolution, not without pain, but with great positive outcomes—as depicted in the evolution from the Agricultural Age to the Industrial Age to the Electrical Age, and on to the Information Age. The present change may well be a part of the evolutionary transformation cycle—in which case, there can be valuable lessons to be learnt from evolutionary theory and business history. Through a great deal of arguments and discussions, we have stumbled on a bunch of ideas, building upon what we have experienced, read about and learnt from various companies. Surely, evolution could teach companies some important lessons!

While working on this book, we imagined that both of us held two halves of a whole. I, Naru, held one half—deep insights into the lives and mortality of new-age companies—and I, Gopal, held the other half—extensive experience of traditional companies. Together, we could reconstruct the knowledge on the subject in a more wholesome manner.

After all, throughout human history and evolution, the younger generation (start-ups) has learnt certain kinds of things from the older generation (grown-ups)—values, life lessons, experience and the art of sustaining a long life. Similarly, the older generation (grown-ups) in turn have learnt from the new generation (start-ups) things like curiosity, adaptiveness, flexibility, a neoteny of sorts where you retain your younger features, and the art of challenging norms.

Keeping Companies Youthful

Neoteny is a word derived from biology, literally meaning the science of youthfulness. It is also referred to as 'juvenalization'. It is about slowing down the process of ageing; it is about an organism reaching maturity, without losing its juvenile characteristics.

There is a fabulous talk by Nobel laureate Elizabeth Blackburn[3] on the subject. It is worth watching because Blackburn was awarded the Nobel for establishing that ageing in humans is caused by the shortening of the telomeres. Telomeres are invisible, thread-like cellular strands that cap the ends of our DNA bundles called chromosomes. Business folks should be interested in this because companies also have telomeres.

Think of telomeres as the ends of your shoelaces, which protect the shoelaces but get worn off gradually. It is important to note that the wearing down occurs with repeated usage, not with time. So why do the telomeres at the ends of our chromosomes wear down? Our lifestyle, our negative emotions, our mental stresses, etc., are to

---

3   Elizabeth Blackburn, 'The Science of Cells That Never Get Old', Ted.com, 18.38, April 2017, https://www.ted.com/talks/elizabeth_blackburn_the_science_of_cells_that_never_get_old

blame. Blackburn says that you can slow the wearing down of the telomeres by practising the following habits:

- Try managing stress rather than getting overwhelmed by it
- Meditate and try to calm the mind
- Maintain healthy relationships and friendships
- Do something for the betterment of your community and others

While no one can deny the importance of money, don't allow it to become your only goal in life. The Grant Study revealed similar findings. Started by the Harvard Medical School with the college sophomores of 1939–1944, the Grant Study may well be the longest longitudinal study in the world on adult development.[4] George Valliant, who directed the study for more than three decades, summarized the key insights as:

- Financial success, at a certain level, depends on warmth of relationships more than intelligence.
- It is important to carry the warmth of relationships into adulthood.
- Alcoholism, neurosis and depression have great destructive power.

The point to note is that there is a science and associated wisdom about how human beings can retain youth, and be healthy and happy. Likewise, as we compare companies to people, there must be wisdom for companies to remain youthful and healthy too.

We are also fascinated by the tea planter's tools and techniques. A tea bush can last a mere twenty years if it is not looked after, but a well-maintained tea bush can yield good quality tea for over a

---

[4] George E. Vaillant, Charles C. McArthur and Arlie Bock, 2010, 'Grant Study of Adult Development, 1938-2000', Harvard Dataverse, V4, https://doi.org/10.7910/DVN/48WRX9

century and is also economical. The tea planter takes care of his tea bushes and loves them by doing what mothers do to their children. Water and nutrients as food, positive soil as growth environment, the discipline of planned pruning of the bush to improve growth vigour, all these and more have been industrialized to give neoteny to the tea bush. The same principles apply to companies.

Similarly, some companies live in what appears to be their original style and form for a century or more, like Tata and Unilever, while others get reincarnated in a different form. The long-living companies do certain things well. If start-ups can emulate the lifestyle and habits of long-living companies, like a person adopting the principles of Ayurveda, they have a better chance of a long life themselves.

6

Companies Are like Human Beings

Companies are mortal and have a life, just like human beings. Companies are born as start-ups, they grow, prosper, decline and die as grown-ups. In case you believe in reincarnation, occasionally, they are reborn as part of some other entity, for example, Chesebrough-Pond's as part of Unilever, Heinz as part of Kraft Heinz, and Lakmé as part of Hindustan Unilever. We seek to summarize here the available research on what kind of principles, lifestyles and habits confer a long life on companies.

Companies are made of people who are hired as employees, employees who have their own agendas, aspirations, attitudes and ambitions. Therefore, companies require to be created and nurtured as though they are human beings. While companies are thought of principally as economic entities, they are also social entities. As social entities, founders of companies want their institutions, which have been created and nurtured with love and hope, to have a long life, be sustainable, healthy and independent. They also want their companies to contribute to consumer satisfaction and their own wealth creation.

In all cultures and civilizations, a person is always blessed by elders to have a long and happy life. This goodwill finds expression in the way greetings and blessings are exchanged: *Ayubhowan* (live long) in Sinhala, *As-Salaam-Alaikum* (peace be unto you) in Arabic, *Shalom* (peace) in Hebrew, *Namaskar* (obeisance) in many Indian languages and *Ayushman Bhav* (may you have a long life) in Sanskrit.

Indian understanding and knowledge about good health and well-being was encoded as Yoga Sutra, a classical text on yoga, by Patanjali, regarded as a saint in India. While Ayurveda keeps the body and mind healthy, yoga focuses on establishing harmony among the body, mind and soul.

Academics write papers on subjects for which they have gathered information and insights through research and intellectual inquiry. Practitioners like us write about what we have experienced and observed.

The proposition that companies resemble human beings rather than machines is contrary to what one is taught when one studies management as an academic subject. Thanks to systems theory and ideas on strategic planning that have dominated management thinking during the last half century, the machine metaphor is strongly embedded in the minds of business leaders. Managers are obsessed with financial models, mathematical formulae and algorithms to predict the future and input–output matrices to help solve complex business problems. By challenging this view, we wish to provide a fresh perspective on how corporate businesses can be viewed and understood—a view that is more organic and less mechanical.

Experience-Based Perspectives

Let us now explore the assumption that the machine metaphor is less valid and less useful for organizations than the human metaphor. We shall be doing this by recalling our individual perspectives on the subject.

In the several books written by Gopal since 2007, he has espoused an overarching theme that organizations are social and human rather than mechanistic entities. In his first book published in 2007, *The Case of the Bonsai Manager*,[5] he argued that analytical techniques and rationality can take a manager up to a certain point but to proceed beyond that limiting space of rationality, the leader must resort to his or her intuition. In his subsequent book, *Six Lenses*,[6] he developed the idea that there is no 'reality or truth' in the world of business: the situation invariably depends on how the viewer sees the situation. He specified six lenses through which managers view every situation, with the result that ten people who view the same data and visible facts emerge with vastly different perceptions of the problem and the solution. In his book on the vital subject of innovation, *A Biography of Innovations: From Birth to Maturity*,[7] Gopal likened the innovation process to reproduction and to raising a child. A concept in the brain is like a fertilized egg in the womb. When the person who has conceived the idea is able to articulate the concept, it is like bringing a child into the world, because for the first time, you can share your idea with others. Comparing the subsequent and well-accepted phases of the innovation process—proof of concept, prototype, production model, industrialization, competing in the market and so on—with the journey of raising a baby from infancy through adolescence and into adulthood, Gopal put forth the idea that the innovation process is a journey full of emotion, and cannot only be seen as a discipline of project management and process orientation.

Naru too has had his own set of experiences in and around the industry and developed his own perspective. Just one century earlier, the average life expectancy of man was barely thirty years as opposed to the seventy years today. To a large extent, this low life expectancy was an outcome of a very high child mortality rate and a high occurrence of infectious diseases. Both have been and continue to be addressed, but as life expectancy improved and infectious

[5]   R. Gopalakrishnan, *The Case of the Bonsai Manager*, Viking, 2007
[6]   R. Gopalakrishnan, *Six Lenses*, Rupa Publications, 2015
[7]   R. Gopalakrishnan, *A Biography of Innovations*, Portfolio, 2015.

diseases came under control, lifestyle and non-communicable diseases came to the fore. In the initial years, corporates too will be afflicted by illnesses that could result in early mortality. Over time, however, corporates will become increasingly better at addressing early mortality, illnesses, and become resilient and strong. However, there is the possibility that a whole new set of illnesses will set in (like the onset of non-communicable diseases). We also know today, that several multinationals and a few Indian companies have crossed the one-hundred-year mark. There are of course outliers who have lasted a thousand years as discussed later in this book as well.

Basically, start-ups as a category have risen to prominence for two reasons:

- They have adapted to the progress of technology that has disrupted or is disrupting existing businesses to find a place in existing markets, or have displaced entire product categories through innovation and created new markets. This fact that start-ups are embraced globally is also an acknowledgement that the time has come for treating this category of business as something unique.
- These organizations are usually driven by one or more hard-driving entrepreneurs who will break many if not all the rules to ensure that their discovery and innovation finds its rightful place in history. We have enough examples of such determined entrepreneurship from the maritime trade days to the colonial era and the oil discovery days. So, this is not something new.

Reverting to the issue of the similarity between humans and corporates, we can broadly say that there is a process of evolution in both cases. Start-ups are like children; they tend to be nimble, adaptive and take risks to get to their desired goals. As start-ups grow older, they flourish by adopting the time-tested practices and processes, including organization structures, of established corporates, in just the same way as children learn to mature emulating adults around them.

From Doing the Right Thing to Doing Things Right

After several years of its existence, during the middling years, a slight paunch emerges, and the start-up is no longer nimble. Following close behind is a new start-up that appears to have the capability to disrupt the middling start-up's existing business. Some remediation is now called for. While this takes the form of medicines and vitamins in the case of humans, training, reorganizations and mergers occur in the case of corporates. This is one of the ways in which corporate evolution happens.

Several Japanese companies that are older than a hundred years suggest that an achievable lifespan for a corporate is at least a century. This is not very far removed from Ayurveda claims that the human lifespan could extend to up to 120 years.

There are some divergences with regard to the corporates-as-humans metaphor. In the case of companies, complete business units, like human limbs, get amputated when they lose their relevance and begin to haemorrhage losses. Humans stop breathing when they die. Companies stop generating cash when they die. Life for humans can end abruptly. For a corporate, it is never so abrupt. One other area where the difference is visible is that while the life expectancy for humans has been on the rise, the life expectancy for corporates has been on the decline.

Although the machine metaphor is common in management thinking, and indeed business organizations have some characteristics of a machine, they resemble living beings more than machines.

- A machine is created by an engineer to do predetermined tasks. Once tested, that machine can continue to do the job, provided the owner maintains the machine in fine fettle, and until the parts wear out. The machine cannot do new things that it was not designed for nor can it operate on its own. It needs an operator to instruct it.

- Humans can do tasks based on learnings and the human is not restricted to pre-designed tasks. Unlike the machine which cannot create its own processes, the human being can do so. Companies resemble humans in this respect. They learn and create new processes just like the human generates new bacteria and cells to adapt to emerging situations.
- Humans live among and with an incredible range of bacteria and viruses, harmful toxins and pollutants. It is a wonder that the human can survive the innumerable life-threatening assaults that occur on them all the time. Humans are able to survive, thanks to their immune system. This is a layered architecture of defence forces that is deployed as soon as an unwarranted or threatening incursion occurs.

There is a lesson for organizations in the way the human body is designed, and the lesson is the opposite of the machine metaphor as explained in the next section.

Redundancy in Human Design

In this context, a talk by Martin Reeves is both instructive and entertaining.[8] He demonstrates that the human immune system has six design principles:

i.   Redundancy: a fallback plan if the principal defence fails for any reason
ii. Diversity: a wide array of instrumentalities to cope with the unknowns

---

[8] Martin Reeves, 'How to Build a Business That Lasts 100 Years', www.ted. com, 14:54, May 2016, https://www.ted.com/talks/martin_reeves_how_to_ build_a_business_that_lasts_100_years

iii. Modularity: biochemical subset mechanisms that can act at short notice
iv. Adaption: not always combatting; changing itself sometimes
v. Prudence: playing it safe; not taking impulsive chances
vi. Embeddedness: recognizing that it is part of a whole and must always operate in harmony

Here is the major lesson: the immune system is effective for sure, but it is not very efficient. Martin Reeves points out an interesting feature of the human immune system—that it is complex, siloed and inefficient. If the human immune system were to be redesigned to be efficient, then it would not have the six features; then we would die much faster. In other words, redundancy, diversity, modularity, adaption, prudence and embeddedness are all essential elements for human survival.

Could the same principles possibly apply to companies? Managers have been so deeply trained to be efficient, rather than be effective, that most of us would hesitate to design systems with those six characteristics. But long-life companies do have such complex characteristics. Companies too have an immune system just as the human body has one.

Companies are constantly under attack from unpredictable debilitating weaknesses—internal control failures, external business risks, human errors, fraud attacks and competition from known and unknown sources. If the company did not have adaptive immune capability, the trends of corporate failures would be much higher than what we experience. Machines cannot adapt by developing their own systems, unless they have been designed to do so.

Management pedagogy and literature are replete with various machine metaphors. Consider notions like cause and effect, predictability amid uncertainty, repeatability amid change, and you can readily understand why managers, deep within, are intellectually aligned to the machine metaphor than to the living being one.

What We Assume Shapes What We Do

We have taken some space here to persuade sceptics that, when it comes to business organizations, the living-being metaphor is very relevant compared to the machine metaphor and systems-driven principles.

An anecdotal validation of our assumption that the human metaphor is highly relevant is an important part of this book because our actions are shaped by our assumptions. Nature teaches us about how strongly assumptions shape actions.

For example, the vulture-family birds, called buzzards, are ferocious when in the air. But before a buzzard flies, it requires a ten-foot run up, a bit like a bowler in cricket. If you place a buzzard in a limiting pen without the ten feet run-up space, it will remain a prisoner, unable to take off. (As an aside, this is quite unlike cricketer Jasprit Bumrah, whose practice spot permitted only a short run in a limited enclosure, and he developed his unusual style of bowling!) Let's take another example, it is said a bat can fly remarkably at night, but it needs a sort of ledge to take off from. The bat throws itself into the air, and most of them cannot throw themselves from ground level.

As we grow up, we learn to make assumptions, and assumptions result in actions as we grow up. This influences how we grow up—and this is true for companies as well, as we will review in the next chapter.

7

Growing-up Challenges

Noted psychologist Erik Erikson charted out in his trailblazing research the eight stages of psychological changes. This was described in *The Biography of Innovations* (2017) by Gopal in the following words:

> Erikson, an ego psychologist, proposed the stages of life from infancy to adulthood.[1] During each stage, the individual experiences a crisis, which results in his or her psychosocial development. The incident or crisis may result in a positive or negative development. The ego develops as it successfully resolves crises that are, for example, social in nature like establishing a sense of trust in others, developing a sense of identity in society or helping the next generation to prepare for their future. At each stage of life, the personality develops in a predetermined order because it builds on the previous stage. Erikson called this the epigamic principle.
>
> Stating the research simply, the key features of the eight stages of life in the Erikson model are:

---

[1] Erik H. Erikson, *The Challenge of Youth*, Doubleday Anchor, 1965.

The first stage is during the first few months of life after the birth of the baby. The child seeks a nurturing and loving environment through which it builds hope and trust for the future.

In the second stage, lasting up to the age of three, the child develops some skills, leading to a nascent but growing sense of independence and autonomy. The parents provide an environment of exploration for the child to try things, make mistakes and learn self-control without loss of self-esteem.

In the third stage, which lasts approximately from age three until five, the child asserts itself through the vigour of its actions and behaviour, and demonstrates a sense of initiative, which the parent tries not to curb.

The fourth stage lasts from age five until twelve, when the child learns to read and write and picks up skills that society is seen to value. The child shows pride in accomplishment and learns to build self-confidence.

In the fifth stage, between adolescence and eighteen years, the child searches for a personal identity. It experiences identity issues through the frustrating search for goals in its life.

The sixth stage is when this child becomes an adult and begins to show itself more intimately, and develops its own unique relationships.

The seventh stage is approximately from the age of forty until sixty-five, when the person settles down into relationships and starts to think of the bigger picture of life.

The eighth stage is what is referred to as the period of wisdom and maturity and occurs after the age of sixty-five.

Ayurveda Principles

The connection of companies with Ayurveda may appear puzzling to the reader. Ayurveda is the science of long life. It adumbrates the principles of how to live a long life, accompanied by good health.

Ayurveda envisions life to be divided into stages and is all about achieving a balance in each of these phases of life as described by ancient Indian texts:

- In the *student phase* (Brahmacharya), it is the stage of learning and the discipline that goes with it. At this stage, we seek enjoyment (Kama) by gaining experience about the world. This is also the period of life dominated by formative forces (Kapha).
- The *householder phase* (Grihastha) is the period for earning a livelihood and raising a family. The primary obligation is to meet one's material needs. The individual seeks wealth (Artha) and is prepared to make sacrifices to obtain it. Fiery forces (Pitta) such as independence, ambition, confidence and sociability are developed in this phase.
- The third stage is the *retirement phase* (Vanaprastha) where the person passes on the reins of the household to the next generation and takes a step back and only provides advice based on experience.
- The fourth is the *renunciation phase* (Sanyasa), the late adult stage. At this point, the person leaves the comfort of his home, renounces all worldly affairs and relationships, in search for the higher truth (Dharma).

Ayurveda cures illnesses by tracing and removing the inveterate cause. Ayurveda prevents illnesses through the adoption of a good and healthy diet. It has been recorded that nowadays non-communicable diseases account for over a third of all human deaths; for example, coronary as well as metabolic diseases that affect humans in their middle age. Ayurveda believes that these arise out of faulty nutrition and adoption of a poor diet, and are best rectified through frequent food measurement accompanied by corrective diet regimes (adopting certain kinds of food and avoiding others), and regular exercise.

Companies too achieve a long life through developing good habits, avoiding bad practices and always seeking a balance among opposing forces.

Phases of a Company

Just as a human being goes through various stages of life, we visualized eight stages of a start-up's life:

i.   An idea is conceived in the brain of one or more entrepreneurs
ii.   The idea is articulated through words and pictures and shared with others for greater clarity
iii. The idea is developed into a preliminary business plan
iv.   The business plan is refined into a pitch proposal
v.   The product and business model are developed for execution by the start-up
vi.   The start-up competes in the market
vii. If successful, the venture achieves its potential
viii. The start-up grows and renews itself to stay relevant with the changing times

Early Stages

An unfettered and imaginative mind which sees no constraints is something that is highly desirable to foster innovative entrepreneurship. A curious and inquiring mindset is a prerequisite as far as birthing an idea is concerned. The reality is that the same unfettered and imaginative mind, which may be a key advantage in the early stages, may turn out to be a disadvantage when it comes to implementation. Particularly in India, many start-up founders lack experience in business and cannot imagine the many constraints between birthing an idea and implementing it.

The unprecedented pace of change, the standard of governance of companies, and finding a balance between free spirit and disciplined processes are all very difficult. Corporate performance in a start-up is usually measured daily, not monthly or quarterly. The measurement systems that we adopt and its periodicity, both can lead to distortions and mutilations at a rapid pace. The investors and analysts translate such measurements into valuations. Both the unilateral adoption of these measurements as well as the periodicity create a volatility that is not very conducive to finding that balance. Commentaries such as in this book may be useful to entrepreneurs.

From the stage of an idea, slowly emerges a documented business plan, often under the mentorship of the early investors or business mentors. Thanks to the evangelization of start-ups by the media and now by the government, this is the most exciting period for start-ups and entrepreneurs. Unlike how they were perceived about fifty years ago, it is no longer considered demeaning in any way to introduce yourself as the founder of a start-up or as someone working with one. On the contrary, such a statement may in fact fetch you renewed attention with a degree of respect because now, the possibility that your start-up could be a success is well accepted.

From a business point of view, however, the statistics are grimmer. Only one in twenty-five start-ups is likely to raise a first round of funds and only one in fifty of those start-ups will reach the stage of institutional finance. Every month brings a new event where start-ups are paraded before an august audience of angel investors and venture capitalists.

Having said that, these are still heady and exciting days for the entrepreneur. No two days appear similar. Many investors appear interested. Only a few progress to the next stage. The entrepreneur is still learning to differentiate between a genuinely interested investor and a curious one. But he makes rapid progress in his learning and is enthused by the attention he is getting.

Development Phase

Our experience has been that a few years of work experience could make a refreshing difference in the implementation strategies and the business approach of a start-up. This business experience need not necessarily be entrepreneurial. What you need is some exposure to the business environment and the way business is done in India. It helps if the entrepreneur has worked in a large, structured organization for some period. It also helps if the entrepreneur has had some management education, preferably after work experience. While these are not prerequisites to be a good entrepreneur, they will certainly influence the way you think and approach problems. And this will enhance your chances of success.

It feels good to be a founder of a start-up. Fifty years ago, it was not so glamorous. All the bright guys went for jobs with multinationals or went off to study in the USA. The entrepreneurial bug bites often while one is still studying.

Your contemporaries may look up to you. During your early years as an entrepreneur, it is often useful to appoint a PR agency to take care of media coverage of you and the business that you have entered. Even a small mention in *The Hindu* or the *Times of India*, will make your heart flutter, especially in the early years. The media loves new entrepreneurs and will try and make their story as interesting as possible and present you in the best possible light. Once this appears in print, your own friends and contemporaries will notice, and you will be the recipient of their adulation.

But these are early days and a successful entrepreneur will see plenty of media coverage in their lifetime. Learn to take media coverage in your stride and not get carried away into trying to live the entrepreneurial dream that the media depicts. As far as possible, share the space with your co-founder. And most importantly, don't start believing the stories that the media writes about you. Those stories are meant to flatter you, but don't get flattered.

A question that often arises is whether the entrepreneur should be alone. Is it good to have a co-founder? Doing business in India can be tedious and exasperating. Eventually, India may change for the better, and entrepreneurs may well be among the agents of this change. But meanwhile, no matter how active and fit you are, no two days are ever the same. It is useful to have a trusted partner next to you whom you can sound out when the issue is perplexing and who will bear the weight alongside you when the going gets tough. And if there are three co-founders, even better.

There is an art in managing your co-founders. It is something that you learn as you work together. Everyone should be conscious that they have to learn to manage this relationship, and they should invest time and emotion to nurture the relationship.

As an entrepreneur, you need to be the all-rounder of the team. All responsibilities are yours, and if nobody else is taking the ownership, then it falls squarely on your shoulders, at least until such time as you figure out whom to delegate the job to. Provident fund payments, GST payments and regular board meetings are the first casualties in most start-ups. Money is always around the corner and it seems easiest to postpone these payments. The problem is that when cash is available, there is always some other more important emergency around the corner. And since these activities do not attract attention on a minute-by-minute basis, they invariably suffer the most. It is best to have weekly cash flow meetings and ask for a highlight of the amount that is overdue on the provident fund and GST. So far as board meetings go, it is best to freeze the dates for a running twelve-month period ahead and inform your board members.

There is also the issue of the pros and cons of starting up an organization and rapidly chasing volumes with scant regard for the bottom line. We are aware that organizations run on budgets and usually there is always an unstated goal of every budget. When an organization is geared for obtaining revenues at 'any' cost, it raises a question of whether this culture can ever be changed back to the norms of a healthy organization. There are some factors that can be severely damaged. How does one inculcate in executives a sense of appropriate product-related marketing expenditure when resources are being committed to obtain market share at any cost? In fact, if Paytm and Flipkart are obtaining market share through perennial discounting and price wars, conventional wisdom tells us that a new entrant can play the same game and upset the applecart once these players have gained ascent.

When visualizing the funding of a start-up, we need to think of the capital-raising plan as one continuous phase:

- Self, friends and family capital
- Angel investment
- Early-stage venture capital
- Mezzanine and growth capital (Series A and B)
- Public issue

Lure of Valuation

There is a popular belief that the higher the valuation, the better off you are. Nothing can be further from the truth.

The early stage valuation is the early reward that the entrepreneur receives for his idea and early definition of the project. Often the first stage should carry the entrepreneur into validating the concept and quantifiable indices. For instance, that the product does indeed sell, and a broad proof of the inputs required to bring the product to the marketplace. This latter is essential for the angel funding stage.

Snapdeal and Flipkart were both early entrants into the e-commerce retail business. Both had Amazon as a benchmark from Silicon Valley. Amazon had pioneered to prove that large amounts of money are required to enter the e-tailing business. They quickly established that they could manage large amounts of funding and that they could execute with speed.

The important thing to note is that investors would like to see the promoters have adequate skin in the game. It is, therefore, that they often allow for a higher than warranted valuation when the company is able to deliver on numbers and on projections. In general, the e-commerce industry assumes that the first mover has a disproportionate advantage. While the company is acquiring market share at a rapid rate, although profitability is not yet evident, investors work on the assumption that profitability will eventually come. This has led several start-ups to demand an unreasonably high valuation.

Investors bestow the status of favoured sectors when they hope that the returns for the winners will be unprecedented. Unprecedented returns become possible when a groundbreaking event is expected to occur. For instance, the successful introduction of the electric car could be groundbreaking in the automotive world.

Arising out of the introduction of the electric car and storage of electricity, there could be dramatic changes over this century in the way people commute and goods are delivered. The changes that a successful introduction of electric vehicles and electric storage could bring about is mind-boggling, and consumer behaviour could undergo such radical change that unimaginable new business opportunities could open. The ability of the start-up enterprise to execute on dramatically new opportunities and the judgement of the investor to spot such entrepreneurs together herald the possible arrival of 'the unicorns'.

But more is not always good.

Start-ups often make the error of either accepting or expecting high valuations disproportionate to what their category can bear or deliver in the foreseeable future. Thereafter, it becomes very difficult to raise the next round of funds, particularly if the entrepreneur experienced early glitches and delayed schedules. Many start-ups have this experience. This is quite distinct from start-ups that fail to take off.

There are several instances where start-ups appear to fall from grace and the only option at that stage is to do what is known as a 'down' round. This basically means raising money at a valuation which is lower than the one last time. The entrepreneur's ego comes in the way of raising a 'down' round and many wait too long before the fundraise happens.

These are some reasons why a high valuation and a high fundraise are not necessarily the best route to success. A high valuation and a large fundraise also suggest that results are expected and quickly at that.

Before the start-up raises the funds and in the duration of the process, the entrepreneur is quick to make commitments on execution. After the fundraise, however, for the first time as an entrepreneur, you have something to lose. Expectations are now sky high and you must roll the dice and pray that your execution is good. At the time you roll the dice, you are spending good money with no guarantee that if this roll of dice does not go right, there will be additional funds to revive you. This is a new experience for the entrepreneur. At the time of asking for money, you were bootstrapped. Now, when you have the funds in your account and the board's signal to go out there and spend, you battle with your nerves. Some of the entrepreneurs will survive this experience and many will not. Accurate decision-making in a short burst of time is constantly required. Can the new entrepreneur manage this?

One of the most useful tools available to the start-up entrepreneur is also the most underutilized. And that is the cash flow statement. If you want to be on top of your start-up's operations, then you must have a firm fix on your cash flows. Are you spending six hours a week on cash flows?

Unfortunately, most start-ups delegate this to the accountant. The accountant is trained to call out the status, but he is not trained to keep pointing out potential pressure points. GST payments, provident fund/ESI payments are statutory payments which must be complied with.

Without exception, in all start-ups, at some stage or the other, these payments get delayed as other payments gain priority because in the entrepreneur's mind, non-payment of operational dues will result in virtual stoppage of the company. Statutory payments tend to get treated like another vendor. Initially, they are small in nature, but over a period of time, such payments accumulate to become such huge problems that they could bring the start-up to a virtual standstill.

But this alone is not the reason why the entrepreneur needs to be on top of cash flows. The cost of an error is very big in a start-up. And therefore, all such decisions that could have big consequences get pushed upwards on to the founder. In fact, in a high shortage situation, daily decisions will need to be given on where payments are to be made and where it can be postponed. Since cost of an error is high, this cannot be delegated to the accountant and has to be taken by the CEO, usually the founder.

Once the CEO starts making decisions on cash flows, then the rest of the organization goes into paralysis. What commitment does a CMO make as to when payments are forthcoming? Should he or should he not? And it goes without saying that once all senior management concern themselves with payments to vendors, then middle management is totally unable to perform. The smallest of decisions that can impact cash flows will begin to move upwards and an agile organization will slow down to the pace of a large, ponderous one.

This, of course, raises the issue of what the founder can do under such dire circumstances.

The decision that the founder makes must appear to have logic. And the organization must be seen to be trying to meet its obligations. And therefore, explanations are called for. And instead of avoiding cash flow issues, as some entrepreneurs are prone to doing, it is best to allocate considerable time to them and to confront the matter. Remember, so long as you are perceived as being fair, the organization can survive an acute cash-flow crisis. But if the CMO is left pleading with the accountant, then self-belief takes a beating, and poor decision-making follows. A word of practical advice that can be universally followed is to go to your creditor before he chases you for payment. We have found that this is a tremendous credibility builder and saves a huge amount of pain for both parties in the long run. And that includes the banker and other lenders.

Setting Lofty Goals

It is up to the founder to set lofty goals for the organization and thereafter ensure that the organization is trying to live up to the same. This goes through at least three stages.

- *Conception*: It is not enough to have a start-up where the staff is dedicated and goes out of the way to make things happen. Working extra hours day after day to make sure that deadlines are met is part of the culture that every start-up entrepreneur tries to build. Making this sacrifice to earn money for the start-up is not enough and certainly should not be a goal in itself. It is important to define our business in terms of a goal that is bigger than that. For instance, a bus aggregator could be engaged in a business where the goal is to 'make the customer's travel more comfortable'. An e-commerce site may aim 'to bring quality within an arm's reach' and so on. And for this very same reason, to merely offer good deals to the customers is not a lofty enough goal. Such a goal needs to be at least slightly esoteric. The founder needs to dream beyond making money.

- *Articulation*: What we want to say needs to be captured in just a line or two. Preferably just one line. It shows clarity of thought. Long paragraphs describing the company's goals are quickly lost on the audience.

- *Reaffirmation*: The message must be repeated, at conferences, at gatherings and so on. As this is reaffirmed, more and more employees will internalize it and this is the first step towards becoming evangelists or advocates of the company. It is important that all the employees become ambassadors of the company and enunciate this in public. Eventually, of course, this message, if well executed, will find its way from the employees to the public at large.

- *Pivoting*: Pivoting refers to a change in the business orientation. Consider how Orangescape and Snapdeal pivoted. That is indeed the story of many start-ups.

Wrigley Company first started by selling detergents. To sell detergents, the company offered a chewing gum as a reward. When this promotion became a tremendous success, the company switched over to chewing gum and confectionery.

Even as Sify aspired and tried to get into the B2C business, they began to realize that this would take a long time and they were running out of funds. They switched attention back to B2B and managed to find a buyer and do an honourable and profitable exit. The new owners quickly cleared the debris of the B2C part of the business and went deep into B2B.

Without getting ego involved, one should be prepared to change the pitch when you face barriers. That calls for swallowing your pride and descending from the lofty statements that you may have made recently and having the courage to dive into the new pivot and still maintain leadership.

Firms that pivot can lose as much as 50–60 per cent of their existing employees, partly by design, partly by default and partly due to cutbacks on overheads while they buy time to recoup. Some key employees may leave since they are disillusioned with the changes in the existing strategy and their dreams were more in sync with the original strategy. Some may leave because they don't believe in or agree with the new proposed strategy.

Overall, it is not a very easy period for the entrepreneur. Nevertheless, he has to single-mindedly chase the new dream and make it happen. He must articulate his new dream with all the conviction and passion with which he enunciated it previously. And this is the difficult part.

To put it more simply, this is the stage where your start-up is running moderately well and your organization is at a mature stage in its life cycle. Growth rates are no longer in three digits and expectations are more manageable. This is also the time when entrepreneurs seek independence, professional acknowledgement and social recognition of their success.

Growth and Broad-Basing

This is an interesting phase of the organization. People might have heard of your organization but the desire to continue to hear about new and diverse things that your organization is doing begins to irritate others. Here is the irony.

For nearly a decade or more, you strove for recognition and tried hard to explain what you do and how you are different from the run of the mill. You might have felt exhausted and demotivated by constantly having to explain and remind people of your identity. But as you hit the householder stage (Grihastha Ashram), you begin to find that folks have heard about and know about you. They may have a view on your business category that you have assiduously nurtured and built. If it is opposed to what you believe, you may find it quite upsetting. Socially, you are now trying to convince people who have already formed an alternate view about your company and its business.

Then you have the professionals, who want to know what is new, and why you don't diversify into adjacent or even non-adjacent areas.

Building an Organization

Readers may have noticed that we have not yet paid any attention to the timespan of the three stages. The reality is that there is no single time period that would hold well across companies and sectors.

Every organization gradually acquires certain characteristics that eventually reflect its culture. During the early days there is a sense of survival and a war-like situation. Sacrifices are made and battles won are celebrated with cake-cuttings and parties. As the organization grows, the camaraderie and the shared joy starts to get diluted. Entrepreneurs struggle to maintain the culture that existed during the early days when teams were small as size begins to take a toll. Valiant attempts are made to bring it back. But eventually, start-ups lose the agility and the camaraderie that used to exist in the early and wild days. And to some extent, it is good to accept its inevitability.

Along with this change, more rules and regulations are put in place. And the start-ups appear to become somewhat less agile and more like the large organizations. More rules mean more bureaucracy and more levels to navigate. This affliction comes to virtually all start-ups once they attain a certain size. And to some extent it is inevitable that this happens. No longer can it operate on the maverick whims and fancies of the founder and it is only fitting that professionalism takes over.

The more dangerous culture that might get fostered in the organization has to do with a lack of profit consciousness. This is especially true in companies that raise capital very rapidly, as in the case of unicorns. In the rush for market share, start-ups often build a reserve of capital that also takes care of any glitches in either strategy or in execution. This usually includes a reserve of marketing capital that can be used to 'buy' market share or match the competition in terms of offerings. When the justification becomes market share, then accountability of marketing and respect for profitability becomes weak. How do you bring this back into the organization?

Delegation and Succession

During the student stage of the organization, the founder is expected to and does become a one-man organization. As the organization matures, the division of labour and delegation of authority assumes significance.

Often, if the organization has grown too rapidly, then it might be in the interest of the organization to bring in a CEO or at least a COO. One of the bigger issues that we observe is the unwillingness of the founder to let go. The issue is not whether the promoter can handle the job well enough or for that matter whether he lacks the capabilities.

Usually, in the rush for market share and survival, organizations do not often think about succession lines within the organization. Several of the senior management have grown along with their organization and have handled portfolios that may or may not be their forte. In addition, they may be reluctant to part with some of their portfolios since they fear becoming redundant. Formal training and development needs should be brought into the organization, and ideally, with the inclusion of external trainers.

The atmosphere in start-ups is informal during the early years. But as the organization takes shape and the numbers increase, the distance between senior management and the bottom layers begins to increase. There are some founders who still manage to display a personal touch, charisma and approachability, especially at occasions where it matters most. This is something to emulate.

During the early years, when rules are still being formulated, administrative exceptions to the rules are easier to make, especially if the founder backs them. As the organization grows, making such exceptions becomes increasingly difficult and often warrants accountability to several tiers in the hierarchy. It is always prudent, therefore, to bring in HR policies at the earliest available opportunity.

This is the stage where the founder, even though still at the helm, makes a conscious display of passing on the baton. This is ideally done when the founder is still involved full-time and can stage manage the changing of the guard.

Stabilization and the New Age

There was a time when time was abundantly available and information was hard to come by. Availability of information and technology was supposed to make our lives easier. However, in the twenty-first century, with information being available in abundance and in an instant—thanks to the ever-evolving technology—ironically, there is an ever-growing shortage of time and life has become increasingly complex. There is less and less time for decision-making as newer information reaches us at an increasingly faster speed.

In this context, the founder has the advantage of having totally internalized the finer aspects of the business that he runs. And for a long period of time, intuition of the founder has a free run. The successor will take time to imbibe the new function. In addition, there is a constant comparison between the founder and the successor.

This is an extremely difficult situation for the successor and a tense period for the founder.

R&D and Intellectual Property

This is a good period to introspect how R&D is to be leveraged and converted into a tangible and value-realizable asset. This is a good time to introspect about what you are and what you are not.

During the earlier stages of the organization, the company would have encountered many opportunities. In the process, they would have also recognized as to what they are and what they are not. Sify and its CEO recognized that although the glory of the Internet was in being a B2C player, this glory was not easily attainable. Rediff.com, which also listed on NASDAQ with an IPO, was a portal and focused on B2C. Portals worldwide eventually shed their glory and withered away. Rediff.com was too firmly focused on trying to make the B2C business work. As they stand today, they have neither succeeded as a portal nor in pivoting. Soon, they may run out of their entire capital, although we must admit that they have a place as a pioneer in the history of the Internet in India.

Governance and Policies

One assumes that now the organization has achieved some scale and needs to be governed more by policies and a competent board of directors. From our experiences, we can aver that long-life companies live long because they have managers who are engaged and know how to manage change.

Two key questions to ask here are: What do studies reveal about the secrets of long-life companies? Are there any generic lessons?

That is the subject of the next chapter.

8

Secrets of a Long Life

If we had to point out the Brahma Mantra of long-life companies, we would say that long-life companies are highly focused on policies, performance and people. And this is the essential message of this chapter.

The only species that can think logically and that can imagine the future is the human species. This has been made possible by the development of what neuroscientists called the neocortex, the enlarged, cabbage-like structure in the human brain. How did this happen?

Thinking and Imagining

Millions of years ago, our ancestors learnt to walk upright on two legs instead of on all fours. This development allowed the blood supply to various parts of the body to be redistributed. The brain began to receive blood differently from how it used to. Over time, the neocortex developed. We now know that the human brain accounts for under 3 per cent of body weight but consumes 20 per cent of the energy consumed by the body. It is an enormous energy guzzler.

As for animals, they can sense an imminent danger, which demonstrates that they have a 'now' brain,[1] a brain that focuses primarily on the present moment. Squirrels, for example, have learnt the value of storing food for winter and remembering where they hid or buried their food from their 'past' brain, a brain that has a sense of the past. Apart from the 'now' and 'past' brains of the animals, humans have a 'future' brain. This means that they can imagine the future where the reality does not yet physically exist.

It is this ability that makes humans curious about the future, and to imagine how the future might turn out: their imagination of the future may be right or wrong, but they can imagine it. Sage Valmiki could imagine the flying chariot called the Pushpaka Vimana just as Leonardo da Vinci could draw pictures of flying machines. It is this ability that allows humans to imagine things that don't yet exist; this is what has made monuments like the Great Pyramids or the Taj Mahal possible.

However, we cannot predict the future with any certainty. In the context of start-ups, we can aid the workings of our 'future' brain by analysing long-living institutions, learning from their experiences and making calculated guesses about the future.

What is it that makes some companies long-living and others short-lived?

Declining Mortality of Firms

We know that the average lives of the Fortune 500 companies are rapidly declining.[2] In the 1920s, American companies had a lifespan of sixty-seven years, but these days it is under twenty years, according to Professor Richard Foster of Yale University. Great companies like

---

[1]   Dan Gilbert, *Stumbling on Happiness,* HarperCollins, 2007.
[2]   Kim Gittleson, 'Can a Company Live Forever?', BBC, 19 January 2012, https://www.bbc.com/news/business-16611040

Lehman Brothers and Saab Motor Company have been felled by economic turmoil or tough rivals in recent years.

In Japan, there are a handful of companies that are more than 1000 years old. Over 20,000 Japanese companies that are more than hundred years old are estimated to exist according to the credit rating agency Tokyo Shoko Research. Long-lived companies are called *shinise* in Japan. Do shinise have a secret formula for a long life?

This is a truly fascinating subject. Over the last many years of close association with various companies, we have gathered some experiences and observations on what makes them tick. There is a lot of research in the public domain on different kinds of companies, from family-managed Japanese companies to American public companies. The observations alluded to in these research converge to a set of common principles. We derive comfort from the fact that the lessons we have drawn from our experiences resonate with these principles.

A corporation does not work or exist in isolation. It is always part of something else, something bigger, an ecosystem. Its very existence and fate are linked with that of its stakeholders. It has a much larger role to play than conventionally understood and practised. This is in consonance with a very fundamental law of nature which states that survival of a species depends on having a mutually rewarding relationship with its environment. This law applies to plants, animals and companies!

It is possible for a person to think that they are always alert to the changes around and yet be disconnected from reality. This is a great affliction among companies.

Let us narrate a story.

Constantly Checking in with Reality

In January 2014, Hiroo Onoda, age ninety-one, died in his native place in Japan. What is significant about an old person dying in his country? Hiroo Onoda was a member of the Mountain Devils, an elite Japanese guerrilla force from World War II.[3]

Almost thirty years after the end of the war, Onoda was found hiding in the Lubang jungles of the Philippines polishing his rifle with fresh palm oil. In 1974, he thought that the war was still on and that he was serving His Majesty's armed forces by staying alert. It was only when he was found by a search party that he learnt that the war had been over for three decades. He was shocked that nobody had told him about the end of the war after he got separated from his colleagues in 1943. Onoda returned to Tokyo in 1974 to receive a hero's welcome.

We mention this fascinating and true story to illustrate that it is also possible for a person or a company management to get disconnected, in their own way, from reality, and become isolated and unaware of the true nature of the environment they inhabit. Like Hiroo Onoda, they may find themselves polishing their rifles with palm oil each morning, getting ready for action.

Good Habits of Companies

Living for a consistent purpose

The world has seen two great management gurus in the last half a century: Peter Drucker (management) who taught how to do things right, and Warren Bennis (leadership) who taught how to do the right things. Creating a purpose and living it consistently through actions and behaviours ensures that over time it gets deeply ingrained and becomes a part of life for all stakeholders, especially employees.

---

[3]   Robert Mcfadden, 'Hiroo Onoda, Soldier Who Hid in Jungle for Decades, Dies at 91', *New York Times*, 17 January 2014, https://www.nytimes.com/2014/01/18/world/asia/hiroo-onoda-imperial-japanese-army-officer-dies-at-91.html

Organizing to deliver a long-term vision

In long-lived companies, the objective of societal benefit takes a higher priority over the individual benefit. This is exemplified in the Tata philosophy and indeed in other long-life corporations. I would like to recall the Unilever approach. Founder Lord Leverhulme once said, 'The task of a leader is to act with the humility of the mason who paves the roads. The man who paves the roads works with his toil and sweat; he knows that for decades after he has finished paving the road, millions of people will travel on those roads. They will travel with hope in their heart and ambition in their eyes, trying to seek out a fortune for themselves in whatever they are doing; but not once will they ever stop to think who it was who paved the road for them—that is the way it is for the mason, an anonymous servant of those travellers.'[4]

Creating an adaptive, collaborative and tolerant ecosystem

We have for long followed the success of Kikkoman Corporation, established in 1661.[5] In Japan, they are known for much more than just producing soya sauce. They have a concept called *kunji,* which means social responsibility. The company set out with some kunji precepts in 1925. For example, virtue comes first and fortune last, and employ the one who deems community life essential and shares the same interest as the community's.

The story of the Intel Corporation founders is also interesting.[6] The more one looks at the three founders who started and ran Intel for the next twenty years after its inception, the less they look like partners and more like a family: argumentative, resentful over past slights, occasionally jealous of and constantly blaming one another,

---

[4]   Cecile Renouard, 'Corporate Social Responsibility, Utilitarianism, and the Capabilities Approach', *Journal of Business Ethics*, Springer, 2010.

[5]   Haruo Funabashi, *Timeless Ventures,* Tata McGraw Hill, 2002.

[6]   William T. O'Hara, *Centuries of Success,* Adams Media, 2004.

and at the same time, they seemed to be tied together by far deeper bonds than commerce. They were also proud of each other's victories, made up for each other's weaknesses, were willing to let go of their personal problems when there was a common threat, and were more successful as a team than as individuals. There was something extraordinary about the relationship Bob Noyce, Gordon Moore and Andy Grove shared, and it was made historic by the extraordinary success that the three of them achieved together.

Most business partnerships—and this is true of Silicon Valley as of the rest of the world—start out happy. Otherwise, they would not start out at all. True, a sizable fraction end acrimoniously, but the acrimony is typically thrown into relief by the harmony at the start. Intel is that rare and perhaps impossible-to-reproduce example of a great company whose founders began badly and gained mutual respect over time. And one of the reasons they succeeded was that they never let their personal rivalries get in the way. They acted as avowed protectors of Moore's Law and in line with their commitment to making Intel the most successful electronics company in the world. It was their commitment that led them to mostly stay out of each other's way and respect each other's turf.

Being conservative with financing

Just like humans need to follow good old habits of watching what they eat, and exercising in order to remain fit, a healthy dose of such conservatism can also lend longevity to the life of companies. In the words of Arie de Geus,[7] author of *The Living Company*, 'Such companies are frugal and do not risk their capital gratuitously. They understand the meaning of money in an old-fashioned way and know the usefulness of spare cash in the kitty.'

---

[7]   Arie de Geuss, *The Living Company*, Longview Publishing, 2002.

Engaging employees

A company is a society of people. It is not an inanimate structure. Every long-life company has found a way to deeply engage its employees with the company; this makes the employees happily walk the extra mile for the company.

Stated simply, the greatest asset that an institution can build is a cadre of highly engaged and emotionally invested employees. Any company can have an assured future if the employees and leaders *love* the company and what it stands for; they will then go out of their way for the benefit of the company and will be self-motivated to contribute to its success. This sounds simple but is an enormous challenge, as we will shortly discuss.

Professor Teresa Amabile of Baker Foundation at Harvard Business School points out that employee engagement often seems like a frill in a downturn economy.[8] But it can make a big difference to a company's survival. It is every leader's experience that lower job satisfaction foreshadows poorer bottom-line performance. Gallup estimates the cost of America's disengagement crisis at a staggering $300 billion in lost productivity annually. When people don't care about their jobs or their employers, they don't show up consistently, they produce less, or their work quality suffers.

So how can employees enjoy their work a lot more? Academicians and Indian philosophers have this to say: create conditions that foster positive emotions, strong internal motivation and favourable perception of colleagues. The future leader has to propel his organization to success, while enhancing the lives of his subordinates. The leader achieves this by offering the employees the following things:

---

[8] Teresa Amabile and Steven Kramer, 'Do Happier People Work Harder?', *New York Times*, 9 April 2011, https://www.nytimes.com/2011/09/04/opinion/sunday/do-happier-people-work-harder.html

i. Progress (give them meaningful work)
ii. Catalysts (conditions that advance their ability to deliver work)
iii. Nourishers (relationships that uplift their work)

Professor Teresa Amabile says that inner work life has a profound impact on workers' creativity, productivity, commitment and collegiality. Employees are far more likely to have new ideas on days when they feel happier. Conventional wisdom suggests that pressure enhances performance; our real-time data, however, shows that workers perform better when they are happily engaged in what they do.

The message is that any institution is a social system. The two secrets to reach excellence are simple: people, people, people, and relationships, relationships and relationships!

Older managers fret about the new generation (Gen Y) of managers. Let's consider some facts about how young folks perceive the organization.[9]

- The communication gap between the young generation of executives (Gen Y) and their seniors (CEO/boss) is wide and expanding.
- Bosses and managers are getting worse at their key task of leading people. And remember that the basic task of a manager is to get work done by being a leader.
- The much-touted emotional quotient (EQ) of managers starts at a certain level in the early part of the career, then improves as a person reaches middle management and then mysteriously, if the person progresses further, the EQ decreases!

There is little point in dismissing Gen Y as brash and impatient; or the CEO/boss as old-fashioned and fuddy-duddy. There must be a constructive effort to bridge the gap.

---

[9] Lin Grensing-Pophal, 'The Training Gap—Desire vs. Ability', HR Daily Advisor, 6 May 2020, https://hrdailyadvisor.blr.com/2020/05/06/the-training-gap-desire-vs-ability/

The support for the widening gap between bosses and subordinates comes from Sue Honore and Carina Pain Schofield's research report from Ashridge Business School, England.[10] The same pattern has been observed in India as well as in many other countries. We have selected only five highlights from the research:

- There is a significant disconnect between Gen Y expectations and the CEO/boss across many issues. Hence, one-third of Gen Y is unhappy with the performance of their boss, and a majority plan to change their employer within two years.
- Gen Y has great but unfulfilled expectations. Gen Y's top three priorities are interesting work (33 per cent), high salary (32 per cent) and career advancement (24 per cent). The CEO/boss has different ideas of what is possible.
- Gen Y wants work that provides independence and freedom. The CEO/boss favours a balanced approach and does not give the same importance to freedom and independence.
- Gen Y wants as boss a person who is a coach and friend. The CEO/boss is unable to shed the traditional superior–subordinate relationship.
- Gen Y wants work–life balance as one of the top five things at work. The CEO/boss gives this much less importance.

The view that bosses are getting poorer at managing people comes from a provocative article by Gary Hamel.[11] He was alarmed by the results of the Global Workforce Survey by Towers Perrin, an HR consultancy that polled 90,000 employees in eighteen countries, including India. One highlight was that only 21 per cent were highly engaged with their work and company (would go the extra mile

---

[10] Sue Honore and Carina Pain Schofield, *Culture Shock*, Ashridge, 2012.
[11] Gary Hamel, 'The Hidden Costs of Overbearing Bosses', *Wall Street Journal*, 28 April 2009, https://blogs.wsj.com/management/2009/04/28/the-hidden-costs-of-overbearing-bosses/

at work), whereas 38 per cent were mostly disengaged. He called this 'scandalous' and felt that the CEO/boss whose job it is to manage relationships and motivation of employees is failing hopelessly— much as a physician who keeps losing patients or a policeman who commits more murders than he solves!

Travis Bradberry and Jean Greaves have written in the *Harvard Business Review* about how EQ initially improves and then, as a person is chosen to lead, it declines in an organization.[12] There seems to be further support from Kannan Ramaswamy and William Youngdahl in their article in the business magazine *Strategy + Business*, which suggests that the boss may be the employees' worst enemy.[13]

In the context of American immigrant communities, Amy Chua and Jed Rubenfeld found that Indian, Iranian, Lebanese and Chinese immigrant Americans are all top earners in America.[14] Their messages probably have some universal applicability. Successful communities share three traits that propel success:

- First, they feel a strong sense of self-worth. Imagine the Indian immigrants in American colleges. The authors term this attitude of confidence and determination as a 'superiority complex'.
- Second, such people constantly tell themselves that they have to work harder and have the opportunity to make more effort. They somehow feel they are capable of more. The authors call this 'inferiority complex'.

---

[12] Travis Bradberry and Jean Greaves, 'Heartless Bosses?', *Harvard Business Review*, December 2005, https://hbr.org/2005/12/heartless-bosses

[13] Kannan Ramaswamy and William Youngdahl, *Are You Your Employees' Worst Enemy?*, Strategy+Business, November 2013, https://www.strategy-business.com/article/00222?gko=ce577.

[14] Amy Chua and Jed Rubenfeld, 'What Drives Success?', *New York Times*, 25 January 2014, https://www.nytimes.com/2014/01/26/opinion/sunday/what-drives-success.html?searchResultPosition=1

- Third, these people strive to postpone their spending impulses and try hard to save and stretch their meagre resources. In the author's words, they seek to suppress the need for instant gratification by 'impulse control'.

Although these have been postulated in the context of immigrants; in India, we call them 'middle class values'. Incorporation of these values could be very helpful in an organization. Once this is established, the right kind of people will join the company and will grow with the right kind of values and motivational drivers.

There is a bewildering amount of literature on how to make managements nimble: sharper accountability, shorter chains of command, flattening organizational structure, more explicit process manuals and so on. Writing on the subject, author Adam Bryant[15] enunciated six steps for management nimbleness after interviewing many CEOs:

- First, make a simple plan that meets the key responsibility area (KRA) test. If you have done so, your employees will be able to have greater clarity on what their key goals are.
- Second, make clear what the larger purpose of the company is. Tata is consistent in stating that it returns to society what it earns from it. Run the company in a way that employees do not feel any disconnect with the purpose.
- Third, treat people well and with respect. Employees resign because of bad bosses.
- Fourth, emphasize the importance of the team but demand accountability and performance from each individual.
- Fifth, encourage frank conversations with employees but without them becoming disagreeable.

---

[15] Adam Bryant, *Quick and Nimble: Lessons from Leading CEOs on How to Create a Culture of Innovation*, Times Books, 2014.

- Sixth and last, meet and foster the human touch. Using only text messages and emails to communicate with your employees can destroy relationships.

It is worth noting that all the six steps relate to human relations, which are things of the heart, and not necessarily of the head. So, is it possible that the secret to dealing with an ever-changing environment boils down to a better understanding and focus on human relationships?

Bad Habits of Companies

Perhaps the most authoritative book on this subject has been written by Professor Jagdish Sheth, chair of marketing strategy in the Goizuetta Business School at Emory University, USA.[16] In this book, he has shown a wheel diagram of the seven bad habits of good and successful companies. Drawing from his research and his book, these seven habits are:

i. *Denial*: These are typically denial of emerging technologies and changing consumer tastes. They create a cocoon of myths, rituals and imagined realities until it is too late.
ii. *Arrogance*: They live on past accomplishments and successes and a strong conviction of being smarter than everyone else.
iii. *Complacency*: They forget that the factors which drove past successes may have changed, and hope to repeat the same successes in the future as well, building up cost structures.
iv. *Competency dependence*: They nurture traditional competencies consciously, and deny the emergence of new ones.
v. *Competitive myopia*: They fail to see new forms of competition, and focus excessively on traditional rivals.

---

[16] Jagdish Sheth, *The Self-Destructive Habits of Good Companies*, Pearson Education, 2007.

vi. *Territorial impulse:* They encourage development of internal structures that reduce effectiveness, such as functional silos, discouraging dissension and missing out on potential synergies.

vii. *Volume obsession:* They pursue volume growth at any cost, missing the healthy balance between volume, cost and customer value.

Each of these bad habits merits a bigger discussion as indeed Professor Sheth has so artfully done in his book.

To summarize our perspectives, when a new venture or innovation is conceived, whether in the womb of a large company or a bootstrapped start-up, whether in the new technology area or in the service area, the entrepreneur must be able to answer certain questions, illustrated below.

Twelve 3E Questions

Energy

- Is my entry and growth ambition in line with my genetic (resource) potential?
- How can I bolster my resources and what will I give up in order to secure that?
- In which market will I play?
- Is that market heavily or lightly contested?

Education

- What will be distinctive about my play?
- What must I do to make my distinctiveness sustainable?
- How can my team be on top of the skill required?
- What should I do to build a sustainable market share?

Eudemonia

- Does my team have stop-loss targets for my company performance?
- What is the path from transactional crisis management to planned evolution?
- What does it take for company leaders to be managers?
- How do I secure the emotional engagement of my employees?

At this stage, we would like to recount the biography of some long-life grown-up companies just to lay bare their habits, good or bad, as practised by them. That is the subject of the next chapter.

9

Biographies of Grown-up Companies

In this chapter, we reflect upon the biographies of some grown-up companies. This chapter will hopefully promote further understanding about the genealogy and life of long-life companies. These are interesting historical nuggets apart from being informative. The chapter is arranged in four sections:

i.   The genius of the joint stock company
ii. Generic entrepreneurship and start-up approaches
iii. Samskara of long-lived companies
iv. Errors of short-lived companies

The Genius of Joint Stock Company

A few centuries ago, every business was a business of trading (buying and selling). To be a successful trader, one had to develop dominance in one or more of these: price, logistics and trust. Price refers to possessing intelligence about the prevailing price of the commodity in various locations, both the raw material as well as the finished goods, so that the trader could sell goods at the most advantageous prices. Logistics refers to the ability to move goods and cash better than others so that the deal could be secured by the trader. Trust refers to the delivery of reliable quality on terms as per the contract so that the customer may buy again.

These competitive advantages were developed and codified within each community and have prevailed for centuries as recorded by trade historians. These communities include Multanis, Marwaris, Kutchi Bhatias, the Moplahs and the Chettiars, for example. These same factors mentioned above come into play when it comes to e-commerce companies. Earlier, the entity that was deployed for private trade was the partnership firm. It had its advantages and disadvantages, but it limited the risk-taking ability to the cash/resources that the trader could bring to the business.

Bigger and more risky ventures in the past, like exploring new lands by undertaking long voyages by ships, were perceived as public ventures. They usually worked on the principle of a charter from the local king or wealthy person. This was the legal vehicle used by the Portuguese, the French and the British traders who came to India and Africa. It is also how those societies developed canals for internal shipping, roads for transportation and railways for logistics.

Trading never offered the opportunity to make a dramatic increase in sales or profits in a very short time, barring the odd windfall, which could well be followed by a bad trade soon after. The opportunity to achieve dramatic growth arose with the industrial revolution. From 1800 onwards, in America, the limited liability firm took shape. This was preceded by three innovations:

1. *Accounting:* In 1458, Benedikt Kotruljevic from Dubrovnik, Croatia, invented the double-entry accounting. His manuscript, displayed in the National Library of Malta, was the first recording of a great intellectual breakthrough. Several years later, Franciscan monk Luca Pacioli developed the idea further. These ideas allowed massive amounts of information to be organized into journals and then be turned into summary financial statements.

2. *Limited-Liability Company:* Stock was sold to high-net-worth investors who provided capital and had limited risk. The East India Company was formed on 31 December 1600 to establish British trading privileges in India. Some years later, the Virginia Company was created to establish settlements in the New World.

3. *Management:* Companies and corporations grew rapidly in the late 1800s and 1900s, leading to management becoming a profession. To provide formal pedagogy, management colleges were established. By the 1960s, management had become among the most prized professional qualifications, attracting thousands of bright students. The world has produced around thirty-five million management graduates over the last century. In 1972, management arguably peaked when Peter Drucker's book *The Practice of Management*[1] displaced the *New York Times* best-seller *The Illustrated Joys of Sex*, authored by a person incidentally called Alex Comfort. This was the way the limited liability joint stock company developed into the powerful instrument that it has now become. Business could now take risks vastly bigger than what the business owner's resources could afford.

Generic Start-up Approaches

Start-ups and grown-ups all follow a similar life pattern when it comes to entrepreneurship. In his writings, management teacher Peter Drucker, has covered these comprehensively.[2] There are four broad entrepreneurial strategies that can be followed, and these are described with the typical American panache as:

i.　Being first with the most
ii.　Hitting where there is nothing

---

[1]　Peter Drucker, *The Practice of Management,* Pan Books, 1968.
[2]　Peter Drucker, *Management,* Harper Business, 2008.

iii. Occupy a niche
iv. Disrupt the product and the industry

If you are the *first with the most*, you are close to betting the farm, taking a big bet and, if it turns out right, you will make a big profit. You just hope that you don't get it wrong. For example, in the 1920s, Roche Pharmaceuticals bet on dominating the emerging vitamin market by paying huge amounts for vitamin patents. Even after the patents expired, Roche still had half of the vitamin market. When the telecom industry opened up in India, Bharti bet on GSM technology and spectrum acquisition. The bet worked in its favour, and the company became dominant in the Indian telecom market. New challenges have emerged latterly for the company, but that is another story.

The second approach is about *hitting where there is nothing*. For example, although IBM made the early 'scientific' computer, it made its name and profits by betting on commercial applications on another brand of computer called the Electronic Numerical Integrator and Computer (ENIAC).

Hindustan Unilever adapted the detergent powder technology to a detergent bar for the first time in the world. The bar market has been dominated by the company for decades since then.

In the third generic approach, the entrepreneur *consciously seeks out a niche* that the firm then dominates. For example, there are relatively small auto-electronics companies located near Fukushima, Japan, and they are original equipment manufacturers (OEMs) who supply specialty electronic components. The businesses are small, maybe with sales of $250 million per annum, but the OEMs are completely dependent on them. This came to light when an earthquake hit Fukushima in 2011.

Marico India prefers to be a key player in the small but specialized medicated shampoo market, rather than being in the mainstream shampoo market.

As an example of the fourth generic approach of *fundamentally changing the product-market offering*, consider how online grocery shopping is gradually eliminating the weekly grocery shop visits for consumer products. When India's Titan Industries entered the jewellery market, the company deployed the carat meter to create a serious and well-founded doubt in the jewellery consumer's mind about the purity of the gold they had until then been supplied by the traditional jeweller.

Samskar of Long-Lived Companies

While exploring a subject like samskara, the reader should expect to go back in time and revisit all romantic stories of times long past, which will then be whetted. It is such a whetting of knowledge that will follow in this section.

In a *Harvard Business Review* article, authors rightly argue that nobody starts by wanting to create a company with a short life.[3] Hence, just as we raise our children, founders too consider short-term and long-term factors as they set up their company. They cite the foundational factors that go into long-life companies as significant.

In a very interesting book titled *Beyond Business*, Pushpa Sundar has chronicled the history of business philanthropy.[4] Prior to 1850, when industrialization set in, economic wealth was possessed by the merchant class; for centuries, it followed a tradition of charity which was informal, non-institutional and on a one-to-one basis. Charity was deemed to be good for business; a desire to enhance social status also played some part. It was also enlightened self-interest; for example, in turbulent times, when merchants needed to be on the right side of the ruling authorities, they resorted to outrightly giving 'gifts' to win favours.

---

[3]   Hemant Taneja and Ken Chenault, 'Building a Start-up That Will Last', *Harvard Business Review*, 8 July 2019, https://hbr.org/2019/07/building-a-startup-that-will-last

[4]   Pushpa Sundar, *Beyond Business*, Tata McGraw-Hill, 2000.

With the advent of industrialization, merchant charity progressively converted to corporate philanthropy. First, because industrialization enabled people to create fortunes far bigger than from trading activities. Second, because it created business dynasties as distinct from successful traders. Third and last, because it created a distinction between traders and industrialists, creating a sort of caste system among wealth generators. This phase of corporate philanthropists lasted from the mid nineteenth century until perhaps a decade ago.

When the history of business philanthropy is updated, we reckon that a new phase will be perceived to have begun with the information technology era. Maybe it will be called the corporate social responsibility (CSR) era! *Businessweek* magazine published a survey of the top givers in December 2003. The survey pointed out that the new philanthropists' demand is for measurable results, efficiency and transparency, and to bring a business-like rigour to philanthropy.[5]

Many of the most dynamic givers on the list are drawn from those who made their fortunes in technology. Several founders are setting up foundations in their thirties and forties, so that they can derive satisfaction by being charitable in their lifetime rather than posthumously. From domestic projects, they are funnelling funds overseas to some of the world's most intractable problems, like AIDS, the shortage of drinking water, primary education and so on. So, a new era in philanthropy has begun, but an old dilemma remains.

On the one hand, investors show increasing impatience to see superior returns. On the other hand, society has increasing expectations about corporate social behaviour. It appears necessary sometimes to choose between maximizing profits and social responsibility. Profit-making is skill-based, while corporate social behaviour is attitude-based. The former represents what you do, the latter represents who you are.

---

[5] 'The Top Givers', *Businessweek*, 1 December, 2003, https://www.bloomberg.com/news/articles/2003-11-30/the-top-givers.

For me, Gopal, spending fifty years as a professional manager in two outstanding institutions, Unilever and Tata, has been a great privilege. They both represent the best in different ways: Unilever, particularly Hindustan Unilever Limited (HUL), which was formerly Hindustan Lever Limited, as a leader in delivering shareholder returns by fair means and with due concern for the community, and Tata as a leader in corporate social responsibility, with decent long-term returns to shareholders.

William Lever was born in 1851. At twenty-six, he started the Lancashire business that became Lever Brothers. At the age of thirty-three, he introduced Sunlight Soap. He never looked back. When he built the Port Sunlight soap factory at Liverpool, he bought 56 acres across the River Mersey because from the very start, he envisaged it as a community as well as a business. This was a bit like the community Tata built up in Jamshedpur. Lever believed firmly in profit as a reward for and as a test for enterprise, but profit was never the chief incentive that moved him personally. Through his will in 1924, he left a part of his wealth to the Leverhulme Trust.[6] Since then, millions of pounds have been awarded to projects and proposals aligned to Lever's own philosophy, i.e. those who combine commitment to the adventure of learning and research with a concern for practical results.

William Lever probably himself did not realize what he was starting when he endowed the trust, just as he did not foresee the creation and development of Unilever within a few years of his death. This would not have worried him because he said, 'The road-maker is the best anonymous servant of humanity. He drives a great broad thoroughfare from town to town, and for generations men travel over the road, with their hopes and fears, with all their cares and joys, never once asking who it was that made their way easier for them'.[7]

---

[6]   Asa Briggs, *The Story of Leverhulme Trust*, the Leverhulme Trust, 1991.

[7]   Charles Wilson, *A History of Unilever*, Cassell, 1954.

Years before Rockefeller and Carnegie, Jamsetji Tata established the J.N. Tata Endowment Scheme to provide higher education.[8] Since then, 3500 Tata scholars have studied abroad, including K.R. Narayanan, Raja Ramanna, Jayant Narlikar and Ramesh Mashelkar. Jamsetji Tata had said, 'We do not claim to be more unselfish, more generous or more philanthropic than other people. But we think we started on sound and straightforward business principles, considering the interests of the shareholders our own, and the health and welfare of the employees the sure foundation of our prosperity.'[9] Those who followed Jamsetji built on the legacies they inherited. Through the years, several philanthropic trusts were set up and have given to the nation a host of pioneering institutions: Indian Institute of Science (IISc), Tata Institute of Fundamental Research (TIFR), Tata Institute of Social Sciences (TISS), Tata Memorial Hospital, the Energy and Resources Institute (TERI) and National Centre for the Performing Arts (NCPA). These are now national institutions.

On 15 December 1969, J.R.D. Tata delivered, in Madras, the Anantharamakrishnan Memorial Lecture in which he said, 'Today, let us face it, the reputation and image of the private enterprise is far from being commensurate with its massive contribution to India's industrial and economic development . . . we must prove to the government, to the Parliament and to the public in general, that we deserve to be trusted . . . we should consider setting up some voluntary machinery for a management and social audit to which we would periodically submit ourselves . . .'[10] J.R.D. Tata felt that the social responsibility of his companies should not be left to individuals; it should be institutionalized. Therefore, in the 1970s, the articles of association of the major Tata companies were formally amended to read that the 'company shall be mindful of its social and

---

[8] R.M. Lala, *The Heartbeat of a Trust*, McGraw-Hill Education, 1986.
[9] R.M. Lala, *Beyond the Last Blue Mountain*, Penguin, 1992.
[10] J.R.D. Tata, *J.R.D. Tata: Letters & Keynote*, Rupa Publications, 2004.

moral responsibilities, to the consumers, employees, shareholders, society and the local community'.

J.R.D. Tata had spoken about the need to complete the cycle; what comes from the people, should go back to the people many times over. In 1910, B. Mukherjee of Lucknow University wrote to the Cambridge economist Alfred Marshall, asking what India should do to become a great nation. Marshall responded, 'If India had a score or two men like Mr. Tata, and thousands of men with Japanese interest in realities, with a virile contempt of speechmaking in politics and law courts, India would soon be a great nation.'[11]

Then there is the Leverhulme Trust, which used to hold a good part of the shareholding of the British entity of Unilever, and spends billions of pounds while ranking in the top ten in Europe on expenditure.

So that is the story of two corporates, Unilever and Tata. Two organizations whose founders lived and established their business at about the same time. These two espoused similar values pertaining to the purpose of business, their institutions—today over 125 years old—have probably far exceeded their founder's expectations by a huge margin, and both of them have professionalized management to achieve 'the stuff of longevity'. Yet, each has done it in its special way.

History, while giving us facts, also creates romantic notions about the past; further, it sheds some light on what we call the samskar of the business. Like individuals, business enterprises too have a samskar. It is the mark of a *successful* business that profits are earned competitively in the early days. But it is a mark of a *great* business that good Samskar get so deeply embedded that they become part of the DNA. A company focused solely on economic matters is like a puddle of rainwater—a collection of raindrops, gathered together in a cavity. But there is another type of a company that is organized

---

[11] John K. Whitaker, ed., *The Correspondence of Alfred Marshall*, Cambridge University Press, 1996.

around the purpose of perpetuating itself as an ongoing community. This type of company is like a river. It is turbulent because no drop of water remains in the same place for long; it finally flows out into the sea, but the river lasts many times longer than the lifetime of the individual drops of water that it comprises of.

India needs many companies with samskar.

Errors Made by Short-Lived Companies

It takes a lot of effort for a start-up to get established successfully. It is like the delivery of a baby, nurturing it through infancy to adolescence. However, the challenges continue; it requires another kind of support from adolescence to adulthood and maturity. Like with human life, corporate well-being can never be taken for granted.

Success in life means grappling with pain, continuous pain.

Perhaps the most instructive thesis about how to remain successful is a book by Jagdish Sheth, titled *The Self-Destructive Habits of Good Companies*.[12] In it, Sheth asks the question, 'Why do good companies go bad?' and then proceeds to answer it by discussing certain deadly habits that success brings with it. To Sheth's list, a few more have been added here.

In brief, these are:

i.   *Denial*: Living in a mythical cocoon of orthodoxy
ii. *Arrogance*: Having a big head before the mighty fall
iii. *Complacency*: Taking success for granted and ignoring the fact that success is followed by failure, as in a rotating wheel
iv. *Competency*: Dependency on core competence and failure to learn
v.   *Myopia*: Defining competition narrowly and not seeing around corners

---

[12] Jagdish Sheth, *The Self-Destructive Habits of Good Companies*, Pearson, 2007.

vi. *Obsession*: Chasing volume and market share to the point of mindlessness

vii. *Fiefdom*: Hanging on to a turf of tradition and culture

viii. *Greed*: Winner takes all, the whole enchilada, and leave nothing for others

There are many books that describe how success was achieved by leaders, and we love to read success stories! But it is also useful to learn how business leaders can have self-destructive behaviours. In our experience, these stories are equally insightful, and we narrate some of these stories here so we could learn from other people's mistakes.

Charles Michael Schwab was an American tycoon at the turn of the nineteenth century. The steel industry in those days was a fertile hi-tech, start-up domain. At the young age of thirty-five, Schwab became president of US Steel, but he quit the company due to differences with the board of directors. He joined the rival Bethlehem Steel and, quite imaginatively, drove Bethlehem Steel into the emerging new steel products.

Earlier, in this chapter, we described the generic entrepreneurial approach of being first with the most. Schwab was an exponent of this approach; he took pride as a risk-taker by believing in the ideology that says if one has to go bust, they why not bust big! In order to pull off the big risks, he had to win lucrative contracts and in order to deliver on lucrative contracts, he found it necessary to circumvent some laws and good corporate practices. He earned so well that he could build an ambitious, seventy-five-room private house in New York worth $7 million. However, the stock market crash of 1929 affected his wealth and ambitions. He had to move to a small apartment, and eventually died in 1939 with a debt of $300,000.

Howard Hopson was a contemporary of Schwab's. He became entrepreneurial and experienced with utilities and was clever enough to 'stitch together' an entity called Associated Gas and Electric Company (AGECO), which comprised a number of companies in New York, Ohio and Pennsylvania, all in the gas and electricity business. AGECO became the largest utility company of its time. Somewhere in time, Hopson became greedy for more and he resorted to pyramid schemes to defraud lenders and stockholders. By 1940, his game had reached an unfortunate finale. Hopson was sentenced to prison for fraud and income tax evasion. He lost his entire fortune of $75 million and died at the Brooklyn Sanatorium in 1949.

Future entrepreneurs would do well to simultaneously learn from grown-ups:

i   the grand rules of success from those who have done it,
ii   how to avoid the self-destructive habits of successful companies,
iii and the ayurvedic secrets of long life from grown-ups.

It is argued, and correctly, that entrepreneurs are infatuated with the 'call of the wild'. They find it irresistible. That is a great calling indeed. But could they combine that calling with the wisdom of grown-ups?

Yes, they can.

10

The Secret Sauce

By now, you have ploughed through four chapters on start-ups and five chapters on grown-ups. It has been a long and hopefully as interesting and insightful a journey as it has been for us. And we know what you're thinking. The question you sought an answer to while buying this book still remains: How *do* we discover corporate Ayurveda? What is the secret sauce for a long life?

As happens with all forms of knowledge, the secret is right in front of us to see. The secrets for discovering corporate Ayurveda too are embedded in the pages of the book that you have already read till here, in the stories that have been shared and the discussion that has followed. The reader must add to these their own experiences of entrepreneurship and management. And there you have it! The secret sauce!

To know how to succeed, one must learn what causes failure and what to avoid. They are obverse sides of the same coin. A fascinating and honest account of how one of India's early entrepreneurs[1] survived failure is *Failing to Succeed* by K. Vaitheeswaran, which is a must-read for budding entrepreneurs. Along with his co-founders,

---

[1] K. Vaitheeswaran, Failing to Succeed, Maven Books, 2017.

Vaitheeswaran pioneered e-commerce as early as the late 1990s. He failed, but learnt very important lessons. In his book, he narrates his experiences with great sensitivity through his fifteen-year-long struggle. The book will be very helpful for aspiring entrepreneurs.

In this chapter, we shall summarize the very essence of discovering the secret sauce to success and building long-life companies:

The Dumbest Job in the World

In 2018, the *New York Times* carried an interesting article in its opinion page on 'the dumbest job in the world'.[2] The key responsibilities in this job were to keep all co-workers alert and alive, to read every book relevant to the role, always appear to be smiling and motivated, be available and on duty twenty-four hours a day and seven days a week, and to be determined to succeed irrespective of how depressing the situation might appear. Finally, the article revealed the job to be that of a mother! And the author was quite right, too!

However, it strikes us that another 'dumb' job might as well be the job of a start-up founder! It is an incredible job that carries all the risks without any clear signs of rewards. Consider just a few of the findings mentioned in Noam Wasserman's *The Founder's Dilemmas* (the data is from a study conducted in America).[3]

i.   On an average, founder-entrepreneurs do not earn more than they would have earned by investing in public markets. There is no premium for private equity.

ii. Although founders see the enterprise as their baby, the majority of founders get replaced after some time, mostly against their will. WeWork and Uber are not exceptions, it would appear.

---

2   Kimberley Harrington, 'Job Description for the Dumbest Job Ever', *New York Times*, 27 April 2018, https://www.nytimes.com/2018/04/27/opinion/sunday/motherhood-job-description.html

3   Noam Wasserman, *The Founder's Dilemmas*, Princeton Press, 2012.

iii. For founders, wealth and power are decoupled. If they want one, they have to give up the other. Anita Roddick, Bill Gates and Steve Jobs are the exceptions, not the rules.

iv. Setting priorities on a daily basis is far more important than in a stressful job because the activities and growth are simply extraordinary.

The list goes on and on. You will wonder why people found a company if it is so much hard work. But hard work does not demotivate a person who seeks fulfilment.

The Dilemmas

A mother faces many dilemmas—an entire book could not do justice to those, let alone a chapter—and the start-up founder's predicament is somewhat similar. The primary purpose of this book is not to educate or counsel the founders of start-ups, though there are a few insights strewn over this book. The purpose of this book is to provide a philosophical shore for start-up founders, the kind of shore that the founder's ship could dock at. Nothing is worse than a founder who is at the helm of a ship that is bobbing in the sea, without a philosophical anchor. It is also important to account for the mental make-up that each founder brings to the act of founding the firm or steering their ship.

As dictated by our own experience, the typical dilemmas of a founder can be viewed as:

i. *Motivational dilemma*: Who am I? Do I really want to do this? Is it compelling?

ii. *Strategic dilemma*: Do I really have something distinctive? Can I create a demand for this?

iii. *Partnership dilemma*: Shall I go alone or with co-founders? Can I share with co-founders?

iv. *Growth dilemma*: How fast should I grow? How much cash is required for that growth?

v. *Relationship dilemma*: Whom should I hire? How much should I delegate?

vi. *Reward dilemma*: How much of the reward should I share?

vii. *Humility dilemma*: How to avoid losing my head? Who can mentor me?

viii. *Ethics dilemma*: How to be ethical? Or can ethics wait for a future agenda?

The list is, in fact, much longer; these are intended to merely illustrate the range of dilemmas that the founder must overcome. Every youngster in the start-up journey thinks that the opportunity is to become a Steve Jobs or a Mark Zuckerberg. The journey is challenging, long and fraught with risks. For those who don't believe in luck or God, founding an enterprise will restore all their faith!

The way new mothers, or for that matter new fathers as well, adapt to the unpredictability, unpreparedness and untiring demands of new motherhood or parenthood, should offer inspiration to founders who are required to adapt to similar challenges. Mothers, for example, gradually learn to generate a third alternative when faced with two unacceptable options. Mothers learn to network with other experienced mothers to solve problems, fall back on intuition when analysis and logic offer no solutions, and plan and dream a long-term future for their baby while frenetically grappling with and solving all the issues at hand.

These are the stages, experiences and challenges that start-up founders also go through.

Discovering Corporate Ayurveda Principles

The basic Ayurveda principle enunciated at the beginning of this book advocates that a balance must be achieved among wind, bile and phlegm in the human body for good health and life energy. Translated into organizational language, this can be interpreted to mean that sustainable organizations achieve a balance among energy, mind and soul of the organization.

Energy is the life-giving fuel or the 93-octane hydrocarbon that fires up society with income and ambition. Energy is the economic activity—business, trade, enterprise—that puts money into the hands of those who can spend the money for the advancement of self and community.

Mind denotes nourishment for the brain and education in society—not just formal education, but the advancement of arts, dance, culture and things that nourish the mind.

Soul refers to the general sense of well-being—health, contentedness, happiness—that comes from the energy of enterprise and the mind being in reasonable balance.

In short, the lesson from Ayurveda and grown-up companies is that if an enterprise can develop its business inclusive of its social responsibilities while delivering a sense of well-being to its stakeholders, it can enjoy a long life. The experience and wisdom from long-life grown-up companies advocate such an approach.

Principles for a Long Life

There are two endearing and enduring books on this subject, one from Japan (*Timeless Ventures: 32 Japanese Companies That Imbibed 8 Principles of Longevity*) and one from Europe (*The Living Company*).[4]

Haruo Funabashi's research in *Timeless Ventures* focuses on long-life Japanese companies and offers a view on their practices as being:

1. Clear in their values and mission over a long period of time
2. Strategic, with a long-term approach
3. Focused on people and the human merit system
4. Customer-oriented and having a sound business model
5. Socially responsible and nation-building

---

[4] Haruo Funabashi, *Timeless Ventures*, Tata McGraw-Hill, 2009.
     Arie de Geus, *The Living Company*, Nicholas Brealey, 2009.

6. Adaptive and innovative
7. Frugal in using resources
8. Ones that cultivate culture and legacy

These statements may read jargonistic, but the concrete and supportive examples of over thirty Japanese companies, which, together, have lasted 50,000 years—yes, 50,000 years—do provide food for thought for start-ups.

In *The Living Company*, Arie de Geus expresses very similar findings with regard to the characteristics of long-life companies:

1. They are sensitive to their environment (as implied by points 5 and 7 in the Japanese companies list).
2. They are cohesive with a strong sense of identity (as implied by points 1 and 8).
3. They encourage experimentation and learning at the fringes of the organization while maintaining a strong core (as implied by points 2 and 6).
4. They are conservative in financing (as implied by points 3, 4 and 7).

Now that the principles of Ayurveda and of long-life companies have been placed side by side, the similarity and harmony between them is self-evident.

In fact, if one were to recall the corporate culture built by the 1980s start-ups, these same characteristics reappear. Think of Infosys, Marico, Biocon, HDFC Bank—all were start-ups just forty-five years ago.

Measures of Success

We conclude with open-ended questions about how and when to declare a start-up successful and its practices worthy of emulation. Is it funding and valuation? Is it market dominance? Is it how worthy it is in terms of initial public offering (IPO)?

We believe it is fair to argue that sustained cash generation and profits are a sure marker of success and reality. Before that, we can only celebrate potential. A question arises here about how much drum-beating should there be about the *potential* instead of *performance* in the real world.

While cheerleaders of these entrepreneurs prefer to promote the exemplars of their fields. After all, there is some value in creating the highly desirable buzz for the enterprise, especially in a society where a business enterprise was frowned upon until just a few decades ago. In this light, one would want to celebrate the potential success as early as possible. This is usually attempted by reports of fund-raising efforts, whereby non-listed entities secure fresh funding at higher and astronomical values.

On a conservative basis, it must be noted that declaring talent or a company as a 'born genius' can diminish the potential of that person, contrary to what we may assume, as Stanford University professor Carol Dweck has pointed out in her celebrated book *Mindset: The New Psychology of Success*.[5]

Tennis buffs will remember a hugely competent woman tennis player called Jennifer Capriati of America. She won a Grand Slam while still a teenager. There was so much attention lavished on her that the poor girl completely lost her focus, and with it, her tennis potential. Indeed, this is also suggested through an analysis of fifty-two years' data of the Westinghouse Science Talent Search winners.[6] Of the 2000 scientists who made it to the finals of the prestigious Westinghouse Scheme, just twenty managed later to join the National Academy of Sciences.

Whether one subscribes to the conservative or the more aggressive view, one should be aware that the exemplary Silicon Valley has expressed a salvo of views since the beginning of the last

---

[5] Carol Dweck, *Mindset*, Random House, 2006.
[6] R. Gopalakrishnan, *A Biography of Innovations*, Penguin Random House India, 2017.

quarter of 2019.[7] Start-up investors, according to this report, have started to warn of a reckoning after some high-profile unicorns began stumbling. So, according to this report, the trend among venture capitalists has turned towards asking start-ups to turn in profits. What a dramatic change from the frenzied rush of start-ups to pursue the illusion of valuation!

'Successful' Start-ups

The 1980s start-ups have demonstrated their models of establishing start-ups as sustainable, long-life companies with positive profits and cash flows—Infosys, Bharti, Biocon and Marico, for example.

Among the 2000s start-ups, only a few have as of now demonstrated these corporate ayurvedic principles. In the course of time, some might. There are those who have established sustainable success as a start-up, and some of their stories appear in this book, like Naukri.com, Matrimony.com and Sify.

In the stories of the profitable, cash-generating start-ups, we find that what we call the wisdom of corporate Ayurveda has been discovered and absorbed to a great extent, and pragmatic learnings from grown-ups have also been adopted. This can be a formula for success for many start-ups and it is to inspire and encourage other start-ups and their entrepreneurs that we have written this book.

We hope you may discover the balance of corporate Ayurveda and are able to make the utmost use of the wisdom that we have tried to extend for the benefit of your start-ups from the experiences of the grown-ups!

---

[7] Erin Griffith, 'Silicon Valley is Trying a New Mantra: Make a Profit' *New York Times*, 8 October, 2019, https://www.nytimes.com/2019/10/08/technology/silicon-valley-startup-profit.html

Entrepreneurs

Entrepreneurs are to the economy like bacteria are to the gut. There are good ones and bad ones, and these need to coexist. Keeping the gut healthy is important by ensuring that the good bacteria overcome the bad ones, but not by annihilation of the bad bacteria. In the same way, society cannot eliminate 'bad' entrepreneurs, but an atmosphere can be created whereby entrepreneurs have the opportunity and incentives to become good or retain and sustain their goodness.

All entrepreneurs work incredibly hard, are driven by passion and impart to their enterprises a massive emotional equity. At some point, they reach the point where returns are diminishing and things are going downhill. That is when there is need for entrepreneurial wisdom and corporate Ayurveda, and we hope that this book offers just that.

In this context, we recall two interesting stories with which we would like to take your leave.

One is from a book written by entrepreneur Ravi Kailas and carries an apocryphal story.[8] Ravi hails from Tarnaka in Hyderabad, from as ordinary a background as you could imagine. By the time he was in his early thirties, he had built the world's largest independent payphone company. As one of the rare successful start-up founders, Ravi made it big and enjoyed the satisfaction of accomplishment. Yet, he also craved for the soul of the entrepreneur. He discovered the power of being an 'awakened entrepreneur' through experiences and stories about Vipassana, the Mauryan emperor Ashoka and Jamsetji Tata. As Prof. Subramanian Rangan, chair at the European Institute of Business Administration (INSEAD), Paris, writes in his foreword to Kailas's book, 'Ravi invites entrepreneurs to aim for leadership in the market and trusteeship in society.'

---

[8]   Ravi Kailas and Cathy Guo, *Myth of the Entrepreneur*, HarperCollins, 2019.

The second story is from a novel titled *Zorba the Greek* by Nikos Kazantzakis[9] and the subject of a fine film starring Anthony Quinn. It is the story of an intellectual and wealth-hungry miner 'the Boss', and the boisterous and mysterious 'Zorba'. The Boss is so busy planning and thinking that he does not quite enjoy himself. Many entrepreneurs are like the Boss. Zorba tells his boss, 'You have got everything, Boss, except one thing—madness. A man needs a little madness, or he never cuts the rope and gets free.' Zorba then teaches the Boss to let go, to dance and to laugh. All entrepreneurs should watch how Zorba teaches the Boss to not take himself too seriously.

---

[9]   Nikos Kazantzakis, *Zorba the Greek,* Faber, 2008.

Acknowledgements

We have traversed a long journey since we shared that cup of Nilgiri tea, sitting up in Coonoor over two years ago. While we had no doubt about our skills, compatibility, our ability to bring our unique perspectives together, we experienced great challenges in fitting these two halves into one composite whole. We hope we succeeded in that endeavour.

If writing a book as a single author requires an effort level of X, then writing with a co-author involves an effort level of X multiplied by two. Despite the efforts and challenges, it has been a joyous experience! Even two people as close as brothers as we are, have to work incredibly hard to put our experiences into a comprehensive and meaningful whole. We hope the output is worth X raised to the power of two! If the reader derives the kind of value from the book as we envision, our efforts would be worthwhile.

So, as co-authors, we would first like to thank each other!

We thank several peer reviewers of the manuscript at various stages. It must have been a chore for them, but the manuscript gained a lot by their efforts. The people who invested their valuable time in giving their suggestions for improving our book are: Srinivasa Adepalli, an entrepreneur; Prof. Tulsi Jayakumar of

SP Jain Institute of Management and Research (SPJIMR), Mumbai; S. Ganga of the Society for Innovation and Entrepreneurship (SINE), IIT Bombay; R.V. Raghavan from Bangalore; R. Srinivasan from Chennai; Anirudha and Nisha from Boston.

Penguin Random House India has been an incredibly patient and diligent publisher. The promptitude with which they signed up for the concept of the book, and the lead time that they gave us to diligently assemble the jigsaw at hand made a world of difference to the book. We thank Milee Ashwarya, Saksham Garg and the Penguin Random House India team for their diligent efforts for this book.

We also thank our numerous sources for the perspectives we got from them. In particular, the conversations—some brief and some longer—with seven out of the nine entrepreneurs interviewed for Chapter 2 of this book. Their candour was so valuable. Other sources have, for the large part, been acknowledged within the book itself. A small part of the material has been inspired by the monthly 'Innocolumn' that one of the authors (Gopal) writes for *Business Standard*. We are grateful for their permission to use the material.

We thank our patient families for putting up with our mental and sometimes physical absence, while we slogged away at this manuscript.

In closing, we thank the entrepreneurs, those we talked to and those we read about. Thank you for being the most interesting and enduring subjects!

Coonoor, Tamil Nadu   R. Gopalakrishnan and R. Narayanan